Dear Jane
with Love c
fra
Pa  x

GOING THE HEART'S WAY

Jim O'Connell MHM

# Going the Heart's Way

SILENCE, SPACE AND STILLNESS IN OUR DAY

the columba press

First published in 2009 by
the columba press
55A Spruce Avenue, Stillorgan Industrial Park,
Blackrock, Co Dublin

Cover by Bill Bolger
Origination by The Columba Press
Printed by Athenaeum Press, Gateshead

ISBN 978 1 85607 650 0

*Acknowledgements*

Biblical quotations are from the *New Revised Standard Version*, copyright
© 1989, by the Division of Christian Education of the National Council
of the Churches of Christ in the USA, and are used by permission. All
rights reserved.

Thanks are due to the Benedictine Sisters, Standbrook Abbey for permission to use the following hymns from the *Stanbrook Abbey Hymnal*
(copyright 1974):

'O Christ, the light of heaven'; 'We bless you Father, Lord of life'; 'The
Father's glory, Christ our light'; 'The love of God was shown to man';
'A mighty wind invades the world'; 'Lord God, your light which dims
the stars'; 'Come, Holy Spirit, live in us'.

To the Iona Community for permission to use the hymn: 'A Touching
Place' from *Love from Below* (Wild Goose Publications, 1988). Words
John L. Bell and Graham Maule. Copyright 1998 WGRG, Iona
Community, Glasgow G2 3DH, Scotland.

To Fr William Hewett SJ for permission to use the hymn: 'Visions' from
*Inigo – Songs and Stories*, by William Hewitt SJ (Inigo Enterprises,
'Inigo's Place' Links View, Traps Lane, New Malden, Surrey KT3 4RY.
www.inigonet.org).

To the Institute of Carmelite Studies for permission to use the hymn:
'Stanzas of a Soul' (On a Dark Night) from *The Collected Works of St John
of the Cross*, trs Kieran Kavanagh OCD, and Otilio Rodriguez OCD, ICS
Publications, Washington DC, 1973.

Copyright © 2008, Jim O'Connell MHM

# Table of Contents

Preface *by Daniel J. O'Leary*                                    9
Introduction                                                    12

## PART ONE
## Reflections for 'Going the Heart's Way'

### Section One: Streams of Love and Living Water
*'From his Heart shall flow Streams of Living Water'*

1.1. Streams of love and living water                           20
1.2. Your River runs deep within my heart                       22
1.3. Feeling our way towards God                                25
1.4. 'You are standing on holy ground'                          27
1.5. A Journey into the Mystery of God                          29
1.6. 'The Father is fond of us'                                 32
1.7. 'God is Love'                                              35

### Section Two: Tabernacle of the Living God
*'It is in God that we live and move and exist'*

2.1. I myself will go with you                                  39
2.2. Life is a the tabernacle of the living God                 42
2.3. 'You were with me but I was not with you'                  45
2.4. The kingdom of God is here                                 47
2.5. The seed grows in silence                                  49
2.6. The kingdom of God – An Experience                         51
2.7. An awakened heart                                          54

## Section Three: Going the Heart's Way
*'When you look into your heart,*
*May your eyes have the brightness*
*And reverence of candlelight' (J. O Donoghue)*

3.1. Opening our hearts to God-with-us in Christ      57
3.2. The heart of God revealed in Christ      59
3.3. The Sacred Heart of Jesus      62
3.4. 'I am gentle and humble in heart'      65
3.5. Love beyond all telling – on lonely roads      67
3.6. Journey through life with Christ      70
3.7. 'Going the heart's way' with Christ      73

## Section Four: 'When Darkness Gathers'
*'May the Light of Christ*
*dispel the darkness of our Hearts'*

4.1. A journey through darkness into light      75
4.2. 'O night more loving than the dawn'      77
4.3. 'When darkness gathers, Christ's love is a fire'      80
4.4. 'Lead kindly light, the night is dark'      83
4.5. Jesus has a special care for the 'Lost'      86
4.6. Jesus was deep into darkness and suffering      89
4.7. God's forgiveness in Christ dispels the darkness      92

## Section Five: 'O Christ, that is What You have Done'
*'O Christ, that is what you have done for us,*
*In a crumb of Bread the whole mystery is'*
*(Patrick Kavanagh)*

5.1. 'O Christ that is what you have done for us'      95
5.2. The Risen Lord – Christ our Light      98
5.3. 'The presence, warmth and light of Christ'      101
5.4. We want Jesus to walk where we walk      104
5.5. The wind in our sails      107
5.6. The fire in the ashes      109
5.7. Within the shelter of the Trinity      112

## Section Six: 'The Unbreakable Bond'
### *'Act justly, love tenderly,*
### *walk humbly with your God'*

| | |
|---|---|
| 6.1. The Unbreakable Bond | 115 |
| 6.2. Love blossoms in a compassionate heart | 118 |
| 6.3. A forgiving heart | 121 |
| 6.4. 'To be called is to be sent' | 124 |
| 6.5. 'Act justly, love tenderly, walk humbly with your God' | 127 |
| 6.6. A grateful heart | 130 |
| 6.7. Hold on to hope | 133 |

## PART TWO
# Living in these Changing Times
### *'Going the heart's way' with prayer and discernment*

| | |
|---|---|
| I. Living in these changing times | 138 |
| II. 'Going the heart's way' | 142 |
| III. Images for Personal Prayer | 148 |
| IV. Discerning the Divine Presence | 154 |

## Appreciation

The reflections and insights in this book have grown out of my experience down the years, some of them out of my struggles. They have been shaped and formed with the help of what others have written. You will recognise echoes of the insights of many writers that I greatly admire. Daniel O'Leary deserves special mention. I am deeply grateful to Daniel for his writings and also for his help and support. Since I sent him the manuscript nearly two years ago, he has offered me great encouragement. He has also written the Preface.

My family and friends have made their contribution to the work as it was in progress – often without knowing it! Their love has been with me in good times and difficult times. To them I offer my sincere thanks. Finally, I thank Seán O Boyle and all at Columba Press.

# Preface

*by Daniel J. O'Leary*

There is a consoling warmth about this book. Like a familiar and comfortable armchair you will come back to it again and again. It invites the weary traveller to sit around the open fire for a moment of rest and peace. But, from time to time, it will also offer some nudges to wake up and get back on the road of our lives with a new look in our eyes, a new spring in our step.

The man who wrote it, Fr Jim O'Connell, is in touch with his own Celtic heart. That's why the book touches ours. His personal prayer-life, his missionary experiences, his wide reading, his childhood memories – all combine to provide us with rich sources for graced reflection.

So many of us will identify with the pictures he paints of our struggles along the journey of our lives, of the obstacles that block our paths, of the hopes we carry even as our energy runs out, and of those childhood days where the seeds of our true selves were first nourished.

Who, for instance, can fail to be touched by his vibrant memories of the kitchen in his Kerry home: 'This was the big room at the centre of the house – so much happened there. In the winter it was the only warm room in the house. The big open fire was constantly blazing. There were no formalities. It was the centre of hospitality. Presiding over all was the big picture of the Sacred Heart.'

He writes about his growing awareness of a deeper reality. 'It was at that time that I began to be aware of the natural beauty and the deep silence of the countryside. On clear days, under the vast expanse of a blue, tranquil sky, I could see for miles west along the valley towards Sliabh Mish Mountain and Castlemaine Bay. The world of nature began to touch my life, and my teenage heart was awakening to the mystery around me.'

This is the world in which God's face is eventually recognised behind every face; the world within which we are all called to taste and experience the dearest gifts of divine grace; the world at whose heart, if we listen closely enough, we can hear the beating heart of God. It is into this world that the author weaves a wonderful web connecting God's real presence with the light and darkness that criss-cross each moment of our daily lives.

Fr Jim touches on many of the central experiences, emotions and memories that crowd our fragile hearts as we persevere along the labyrinths of our days. He is sure-footed and consoling as he brings his holy, wholesome and homely wisdom to bear on the loneliness, despair, hope, loss, forgiveness and dreams that most of us experience. He has a deep sense of the humanity of Jesus and of the compassion of a 'loving God who is always near us, with us and even in us. Human beings are now home to God, the infinite mystery. Ordinary human life is shot through with God's presence, God's light and God's love.'

There is an inner authority about these reflections. The scripture passages, the prayers, the reflections, the songs and hymns – all provide a lasting nourishment for busy, anxious or lonely people. They are offered to us humbly and simply, in an open invitation, to choose, to linger, to skip, to return to, as the Spirit moves us.

Those who are committed to following the way of the heart will find it helpful to prepare for their daily engagement with God in a number of ways. It is recommended to have a favourite chair or cushion in a suitably quiet place in the house. A small ritual such as a bow before beginning, the lighting of a candle, the relaxing of the breath and body helps to place us in the right frame of mind and heart. It certainly seems advisable to keep a fixed time each day for the precious moment of reflection.

The thoughts, suggestions, quotations, selections and meditations in *Going the Heart's Way* are all solidly grounded in a spirituality of humanity, in a theology of nature and grace, and in a Celtic tradition. They spring from a clear vision of incarnation when God took delight in becoming human exactly like us. This humanity of Jesus, with its strong emotions, passions, temptations and doubt, shines through every page of this book. It is our humanity too. We take heart therefore from the wonderful good news that we are all made in God's image.

'The Holy Spirit fills our sails and powers us forward on our journey into the depths of the mystery of God – a God who hovers in love over us when we are bruised and broken, when our hearts are troubled and our souls are weary.' May this blessed book bring light to your darkness, hope to your despair, and joy to your sorrow. May it comfort and console you like an angel from God. May it purify, celebrate and deepen your own 'one wild and precious life'.

*Daniel J. O'Leary*

# Introduction

I was born to a farming family near the village of Scartaglen, in the Sliabh Luachra area of east Kerry. Although the land around there is poor for the most part, the landscape is pleasing to the eye and gentle on the soul. A river runs through it, and there are lots of rolling hills, wooded valleys, streams and glens. The river is the Brown Flesk, and it has a special place in my memory. In the summer season, stretches of it were hidden under a dense blanket of green willows, and its banks were covered with flowers: daffodils, bluebells, primroses, daisies, violets, buttercups and many other varieties. For my young eyes, it was full of beauty and mystery. I was fascinated by it. But there was also fear of the river. We were constantly warned to keep well away from it, though we did not always heed the warning. In later years I often smiled at its gentleness, when I walked along its banks and realised it was very much in its infancy at that stage of its journey to the sea.

## A Window of Wonder

During my teenage years, life was difficult. I spent a lot of time working in the fields with my father and my brothers. The work was hard, especially during the summer months. Like every teenage boy, I was dealing with the issues of identity and sexuality, and, at that time, there was no sharing or discussion about such matters. I was also worried about the future; in the Ireland of the late nineteen fifties, there was little chance of further education and the prospects of getting a job were not great.

But something else was happening for me during those years. A little window of wonder began to open, and I became aware of the natural beauty and the deep silence of the countryside. There were places on our farm where I found a great sense of space and stillness. On clear days, under the vast expanse of a blue tranquil sky, I could see for miles west along the valley towards Sliabh Mish Mountain and Castlemaine Bay. On calm nights, I often lingered outside, standing there alone in the stillness of the night, listening to the murmur of the river and the ripple of the streams, very much aware of the silence and the solitude. I was moved and attracted by what I felt and saw and heard on those nights and days long ago. The world of nature began to touch my life, and my teenage heart was awakening to the mystery around me.

### 'Going the Soul's Way' ('the Heart's Way')

I may not have realised it at the time but, in its own humble way, my early experience of nature was an awakening to the mystery of God's presence. This was something that affected me deeply, and, to a large extent, determined the direction of my life from then on. I have tasted and glimpsed this kind of experience on many occasions down the years. As the great English poet, William Wordsworth, wrote: 'Nature never did betray the heart that loved her.' That line expresses what I have often known and felt. So too do these lines from John Moriarty:

> Clear Days bring the mountains
> right down to my doorstep,
> Calm nights give the rivers their say,
> The wind puts its hand to my shoulder some evenings,
> And then I don't think,
> I just leave what I am doing and I go the soul's way.[1]

Here we have a good description of what happens when the world of nature touches us deeply and opens our souls and our hearts to the mystery that surrounds us. On clear days and calm nights the beauty of creation can awaken our hearts and souls; it could be the sound of the river, the sight of the mountain, the flight of the swallow, the gentle breeze, the smell of new mown

1. John Moriarty, *Nostos*, Lilliput Press, Dublin, 2001, p 491.

grass, or the torrent of the waterfall that moves us to a deeper level. With a sense of presence and peace, we are drawn to leave what we are doing and 'go the soul's way' ('the heart's way'). In this context, the 'soul's way' and the 'heart's way' describe much the same experience. I have chosen to use 'the heart's way.'

Close contact with nature helps us to 'go the heart's way,' but so too do music, poetry, art and friendship. Any, or indeed all of these, can touch our hearts and help us to engage with mystery. There are so many things in life that can do this. Just look at a little child; the perfection and fragility of the tiny body at birth can leave us full of wonder, while the smile of an infant in its mother's arms tells a story of love, comfort, security and mystery.

We can get a glimpse of mystery in the most ordinary experiences of life since: 'Life is a tabernacle of the living God' (Joan Chittester). I remember people of my parents' generation expressing their sense of God's closeness in the words of an Irish saying that translates as: 'The help (presence) of God is nearer than the door.' God is much nearer than the door, present deep within our hearts and in the fabric of ordinary human living. When we 'go the heart's way' we can sometimes feel that presence but, of course, we will not feel it in a definite way all the time. In everyone's life, there is light and darkness, and there are plenty of doubts and difficulties along the way.

## 'A Safer Way of Drawing Nigh unto God'

All forms of Christian prayer, liturgy, scripture and the sacraments have special significance for 'going the heart's way' into the mystery of God. They can take us further and deeper. Shortly before he died, John Moriarty wrote: 'Unlike so many Romantic poets, I couldn't be content with the natural liturgy of lake water lapping, or with the natural sounds, just sounds, of linnets' wings. The truth is, I once was. Indeed, for three years in Connemara I was rapturously content with them … But then there was a day when it only took one small lap of Loch Inagh water and not only were the mirrored mountains gone, the world was gone, and I was in a void that I didn't immediately or soon afterwards recognise to be God in his enduring mode as Divine *Mirum'* (wonder, miracle, mystery). This experience was the beginning of a long journey for John that led him back to Christianity, which he had abandoned earlier in life. In his later years, he discovered that Christian prayer, liturgy, scripture and the sacraments bring us into contact with God in a very special way; they shelter us on our journey through the mystery, and 'they are a safe or at the very least a safer way of drawing nigh unto God.'

Quiet time in personal prayer is one of the forms of Christian prayer that can be a great help to us on our journey. In the silence, the heart is awakened to the reality of God present to us in the world of nature, in the midst of human life and in the depths of the human heart: 'Indeed God is not far from each one of us, since it is in him that we live and move and have our being' (Acts 17:28).

The heart's awakening often happens quietly. There is no great fanfare. There is just the calm journey through the days and years and the effort to remain faithful to quiet time in prayer. If we manage this, the window of the heart begins to open to the mystery of God in ordinary life, and human experience lights up with a light that leads to God. In Patrick Kavanagh's words:

> 'Child there is light somewhere under a star,
> Sometime it will be for you
> A window that looks inward to God'

## PART ONE:
## Reflections for 'Going the Heart's Way'

Some of the reflections in Part One started life as short papers that I prepared for people who wanted to spend quiet time in prayer. I was involved in this work over a period of twelve years that I spent in Kenya. Those who used the reflections told me that they found them helpful. This encouraged me to do more work on them. And, as often happens, they took on a life of their own, and I ended up with this book. My modest hope is that the reflections will be of help to anyone who is interested in personal prayer. In a more general way, the reflections can be read with a view to getting a better understanding of some of the central areas of our Christian Faith.

There are forty-two reflections, divided into six sections. They cover various aspects of the journey of faith. In each reflection, I begin with some thoughts on the theme presented. Then you will find a selection of scripture passages, psalms and hymns. The selection is personal. You may have your own selection, or you may want to avail of all the other helps, like music, poetry and so on.

Many of the readings, psalms and hymns presented in the reflections have sustained me over the years and helped me on my own journey. I hope they will do the same for you. I have found myself going back, time and again, to some of the same passages. It is like going to draw water from the same well day after day. You may find that the same thing happens for you. There is no need to cover everything. A short reading of scripture, even one verse, with the touch of the Spirit, can keep us going for a long time.

### Belief in a Loving God

Running through the reflections is a belief in a loving God who is always near us, with us and even in us. We believe that 'The Word was made flesh and lives among us' (Jn 1:14), and 'Jesus is Immanuel, a name that means 'God-is-with-us' (Mt 1:23). Human life and human beings are now home to God, the infinite mystery. Ordinary human experience is shot-through with God's presence, God's light and God's love: 'Earth is crammed with Heaven, and every common bush is afire with God' (E. B. Browning). This image describes rather well our belief in the nearness of God (God's presence with us), which goes hand in hand with respect for the eternal mystery of God, who is always beyond us.

For many people, belief in a loving God does not come easily, especially in the face of so much suffering in the world. Yet we are assured that the spiritual journey is the story of the human heart opening up to the mystery of this loving God – a God who reaches out to us and draws us into his life and love. In the words of St Augustine, 'We are being drawn by the bonds of love that only lovers would understand' and 'God hovers in love over the fragments of our brokenness, over the dark and storm-tossed waters God hovers in mercy.' Augustine described his own experience in these words: 'It was as if a soft peaceful light (God's light and love) flowed into my heart, and all the dark shadows fled away.'

What a difference it would make if we could truly believe in this loving God: a God who hovers in love over us when we are bruised and broken, when our hearts are troubled and our souls are weary; a God who is like the merciful father welcoming home his lost son; a God who is like the good shepherd who goes off in search of the lost sheep; and a God who is like the woman who turns the house up-side-down searching for a lost coin. Here we have deep insights into the nature of God, the heart of God, who loves us so much that he sent his only Son into the world to be our Saviour (Jn 3:16).

PART TWO:
### Living in these changing times

### 'Going the Heart's Way' with Discernment and Prayer

Part Two begins with a short reflection on living in these changing times, and the need to have some quiet time (take a breather!) in our day. This is followed by some insights into 'Going the Heart's Way.' Then you will find a description of images for personal prayer. These images offer insights into the nature of prayer and its importance for our journey to God. The final section is a short article on Discerning the Divine Presence. This is a very important but also a very complex topic. When we 'go the heart's way' we need to read the signs that will take us in the right direction. With the help of discernment, we learn to be more sensitive to the presence of the Holy Spirit working in our hearts, in our lives and in our world.

PART ONE

# Reflections for 'Going the Heart's Way'

Contemplative Prayer is a gaze of faith fixed on Jesus …
His gaze purifies our hearts;
the light of his countenance illumines the eyes of our hearts
and teaches us to see everything
in the light of his truth and his compassion for all people'
(CCC 2715)

If we make this contemplative habit of mind and heart
like second nature to us,
the time we spend alone with God in personal prayer
will be rich and transforming.
(Daniel J. O' Leary, Travelling Light)

PART ONE: SECTION ONE
## Streams of Love and Living Water
*'From his Heart shall flow Streams of Living Water'*
(Jn 7:38)

## 1.1. Streams of love and living water

Water, wells, streams, springs and rivers provide us with lasting and familiar images. They are often used in the Bible to describe aspects of the journey into the mystery of God. In Psalm 41 we pray: 'As a deer longs for flowing streams, so my soul longs for you, O God.' In Isaiah 12:3 we read: 'With joy you will draw water from the wells of salvation.' And the very first psalm tells us that a good person is like a tree that is planted by streams of water, which yields its fruit in due season.

Jesus himself, in his conversation with the woman at the well, says: 'The water that I shall give will become a spring of water, gushing up to eternal life.' So try to imagine God's love flowing constantly like a great stream or river in our hearts. This stream of love rises in the heart of God, as a spring of living water and flows out into you and me. This is what we believe. This is what scripture tells us again and again: 'By the tender mercy of our God, the dawn from on high will break upon us, to give light to those who sit in darkness and in the shadow of death, to guide our feet into the way of peace' (Lk 1:68-79).

We want to be as open as possible to the stream of God's love, so that we can have the experience of being drawn into it and swept along by it. Let us pray that this will happen. Let us hope that in the midst of the busy hectic world of daily life we will be in touch with God's loving presence in silence and peace.

*Please read the following slowly and prayerfully and remember that: 'The scriptures are not to be read in noisy situations, but where things are quiet, not cursorily and at a rush, but a little at a time, with intent and lingering meditation' (St Anselm).*

*John 4:5-15*

Jesus, tired out by his journey, was sitting by Jacob's well. It was about noon. A Samaritan woman came to draw water, and Jesus said to her, 'Give me a drink.' (His disciples had gone to the city to buy food.) The Samaritan woman said to him, 'How is it that you, a Jew, ask a drink of me, a woman of Samaria?' Jesus answered her, 'If you knew the gift of God, and who it is that is saying to you, "Give me a drink," you would have asked him, and he would have given you living water.' The woman said to him, 'Sir, you have no bucket, and the well is deep. Where do you get that living water? Are you greater than our ancestor Jacob, who gave us the well, and with his sons and his flocks drank from it?' Jesus said to her, 'Everyone who drinks of this water will be thirsty again, but those who drink of the water that I will give them will never be thirsty. The water that I will give will become in them a spring of water gushing up to eternal life.' The woman said to him, 'Sir, give me this water, so that I may never be thirsty or have to keep coming here to draw water.'

*Psalm 42*
*(With the psalmist we recognise our need and our thirst for God)*

As a deer longs for flowing streams,
so my soul longs for you, O God.
My soul thirsts for God,
for the living God.

When shall I come and behold the face of God?
Why are you cast down, O my soul,
and why are you disquieted within me?
Hope in God; for I shall again praise him,
my help and my God.

Deep calls to deep at the thunder of your cataracts;
all your waves and your billows have gone over me.
By day the Lord commands his steadfast love,
and at night his song is with me,
a prayer to the God of my life.

## 1.2. 'Your River runs deep within my heart'

The human heart is the sanctuary of God's love: God's love has been poured into our hearts through the Holy Spirit that has been given to us (Rom 5:5). The stream or river of God's love is flowing deep within us. It flows night and day, while we sleep, while we are awake – how we do not know. This image helps us to get some grasp of the mystery of God's love. This is the love that we are being drawn into, so that we can soak ourselves in it and steep ourselves in it. In St Paul's words, Christ lives in our heart through faith and we are planted in love and built on love.

We have to remember that we are using an image when we talk about the river or stream. Like all images, if we take it too literally we may end up disappointed. Of course, if you are blessed with a sense of the river or stream of love flowing in your heart, then thank God for it. You can desire it and pray for it. But this may not be the way it is for you. It is usually much less dramatic. The river of love flows softly and gently and silently. St Ignatius of Loyola said grace (love) is delicate, gentle, and delightful. It can be compared to a drop of water penetrating a sponge. It does not clatter 'like a drop of water falling on a stone.' So be open to the possibility of it happening this way for you. We may not even notice God's love and grace unless we grow accustomed to looking for it and praying for it.

*Please read the following scripture passage and hymn slowly and prayerfully. Take time. Do not rush. Ask God to help you to experience his love flowing deep within your heart.*

*Ephesians 3:14-21*
For this reason I bow my knees before the Father of our Lord Jesus Christ, from whom every family in heaven and on earth takes its name. I pray that, according to the riches of his glory, he may grant that you may be strengthened in your inner being with power through his Spirit, and that Christ may dwell in your hearts through faith, as you are being rooted and grounded in love. I pray that you may have the power to comprehend,

with all the saints, what is the breadth and length and height and depth, and to know the love of Christ that surpasses knowledge, so that you may be filled with all the fullness of God. Now to him who by the power at work within us is able to accomplish abundantly far more than all we can ask or imagine, to him be glory in the church and in Christ Jesus to all generations, forever and ever. Amen.

Hymn[2]
*(This Hymn is based on the writings of St Ignatius. It is rich in images. The river of God's love keeps flowing for each person on the journey through life: 'Your River runs deep along my road ... Your River runs deep within my heart'.)*

The Father loves the Son with all the love he is;
The Son responds with loving as total as his;
The Spirit is the living love of Father and Son,
Receiving and giving their three love as one.

How can a love so total say anything to me?
How can love be so selfless – so totally free?
How can love be a spirit our eyes cannot see?
How can love speak love's meaning to you and to me?

The love of the Father took flesh in the Son;
The love of the Son still lives on his friends;
The love of the Spirit is born in each heart,
Awaiting, awakening when rocks break apart.

Lord Jesus Christ, my King, my Sun,
You are the source whence love's rays come;
You shine through all things, your loving flows.
Through bread and wine, your presence grows.

I sense your light in every ray;
I see you shape each break of day;

2. From: *Inigo – Songs and Stories*, by William Hewitt SJ (Inigo Enterprises, 'Inigo's Place' Links View, Traps Lane, New Malden, Surrey KT3 4RY. www.inigonet.org)

In Bread and Wine though our eyes can't see,
I sense your love enliven me.

I see your rays one with the sun;
I see them reach to everyone;
In Bread and Wine Lord remembered be;
transform our lives, Lord make us free.

The river runs deep along my road;
it hums its song, makes light my load;
It leads me on beyond my fears;
it opens locks, releases tears.

Your river runs deep within my heart
releases springs in deepest parts.
It leads me on to spaces new,
it opens gates, lets flow what's true.

Our river runs deep, my heart is full,
your song flows through each depth I feel;
I know you are here wherever I go:
Lord, may our river ever flow.

## 1.3. Feeling our way towards God

Scripture tells us that: 'God made all nations to inhabit the whole earth ... so that they would search for God, and perhaps grope for him and find him – though indeed he is not far from each one of us. For in him we live and move and have our being' (Acts 17:27-28). If we reflect on these verses of scripture, we come to realise how important the heart and feelings are on our journey to God. Some translations use the words 'by feeling their way to God, people will find him'. The affective, experiential area of life is central. It is all about opening the heart to the mystery of God's love and presence. This is why images and symbols, as well as parables and metaphors, are so important. They touch and reach into feelings and emotions in a way that human thinking can never do. They engage the heart, the soul, the spirit and the whole being. So, in a sense, we have to feel our way towards God.

Sometimes the feelings can be strong, with a deep sense of God's presence, while at other times there is only a whisper or touch of God. Spiritual writers tell us that this is often the way it is; this is God's way of revealing himself to us. For most people there are no great shining lights and visions but God's loving presence is being made manifest in a quiet way, in our hearts, in our lives and in our world. We can come to realise this as we experience the sense of mystery in our lives. 'Feeling' and 'Noticing' are key words. Through faith we can feel and notice God's presence and open our hearts to his beauty and love. This is the spark that makes our ordinary humdrum lives light up with God.

*Please read the following scripture passage and psalm slowly and prayerfully. You may want to read them more than once. Then you can pick out some of the verses or phrases that have touched you deeply. Let them sink into your heart and being. Take time. Do not rush. Ask for the grace to 'feel your way towards God.'*

*Acts 17:24-28*

The God who made the world and everything in it, he who is Lord of heaven and earth, does not live in shrines made by human hands, nor is he served by human hands, as though he needed anything, since he himself gives to all mortals life and breath and all things. From one ancestor, he made all nations to inhabit the whole earth ... so that they would search for God, and perhaps grope for him and find him – though indeed he is not far from each one of us. For 'In him we live and move and have our being.'

*Psalm 23*
*(In this psalm, the shepherd image expresses God's loving presence with us.)*

> The Lord is my shepherd, I shall not want.
> He makes me lie down in green pastures;
> he leads me beside still waters; he restores my soul.
>
> He leads me in right paths, for his name's sake.
> Even though I walk through the darkest valley,
> I fear no evil; for you are with me;
> your rod and your staff – they comfort me.
>
> Surely goodness and mercy shall follow me
> all the days of my life,
> and I shall dwell in the house of the Lord
> my whole life long.

## 1.4. 'You are standing on holy ground'

The image of 'standing on holy ground' comes to us from the passage in the Book of Exodus which describes the experience of Moses on Mount Horeb, the mountain of God. (Exodus 3:1-6). From there too comes the image of 'the burning bush'. God appeared to Moses in a flame blazing from the middle of a bush. When Moses looked, he saw the bush was blazing but it was not being burnt up. So he decided to investigate. As Moses approached the bush, God said to him: 'Take off your shoes, for the place where you are standing is holy ground' (Ex 3:5-6).

So the 'the burning bush' becomes a symbol of God's presence at the heart of nature and of life. In a sense every bush burns. The stream of God's loving presence keeps flowing through all the events and experiences of life. Wherever we are, the place where we stand is 'holy ground'. You can meet and recognise God's presence there. It is very important to notice what we experience and what is happening before our eyes. There are so many acts of kindness and love that we do not notice. Perhaps we need to train ourselves to be more aware of the goodness that shines through the simplest events and experiences in our lives. Even very ordinary experiences can be an opening to the mystery of God. In the words of the Irish poet, Patrick Kavanagh, 'the ordinary has special wings'. The whisper or touch of God is all around us. You are standing on holy ground wherever you are. God is found or met where we live our lives, often complicated, confused and perhaps sometimes chaotic. Through faith we can recognise and encounter God in our ordinary lives. Faith opens our hearts to the beauty of God; it is like a spark that can make our lives light up with God.

*Please read the following slowly and prayerfully and ask for the faith to open your heart to the mystery of God at the heart of nature and in the events and experiences of your ordinary daily life.*

*Exodus 3:1-7*

Moses was keeping the flock of his father-in-law Jethro, the priest of Midian; he led his flock beyond the wilderness, and came to Horeb, the mountain of God. There the angel of the Lord appeared to him in a flame of fire out of a bush; he looked, and the bush was blazing; yet it was not consumed. Then Moses said, 'I must turn aside and look at this great sight, and see why the bush is not burned up.' When the Lord saw that he had turned aside to see, God called to him out of the bush, 'Moses, Moses!' And he said, 'Here I am.' Then he said, 'Come no closer! Remove the sandals from your feet, for the place on which you are standing is holy ground.' He said further, 'I am the God of your father, the God of Abraham, the God of Isaac, and the God of Jacob.' And Moses hid his face, for he was afraid to look at God.

*Psalm 139:*
*(This Psalm expresses a tremendous sense of God's loving presence, God's closeness. God knows all about us. God is with us wherever we go, whatever we do and wherever we are.)*

O Lord, you have search me and known me.
You know when I sit down and when I rise up;
You discern my thoughts from far away.

Where can I go from your Spirit?
Or where can I flee from your presence?
If I take the wings of the morning
and settle at the farthest limits of the sea,
even there your hand shall lead me,
and your right hand shall hold me fast.

Search me, O God, and know my heart;
test me and know my thoughts.
See if there is any wicked way in me,
and lead me in the way everlasting.

## 1.5. A Journey into the Mystery of God

I want to introduce another image that is very familiar to us: the image of being on a journey. It is helpful to describe the life of faith as a journey into the mystery of God – into the mystery of God's light and love, into God's presence and peace. It is a special kind of journey. The image of a being on a journey describes the day-to-day movement of the person as he or she grows in the love of God, and lives this out in love of self, others and creation.

We believe that it is a journey to the centre of love, because God is love. It is a journey of a life being lived at a deeper level. It is like being drawn by a magnet towards the centre, towards the heart of God, which is the source of the stream of love.

As a migrating bird has its own inner instinct or radar that it follows, we have a desire for God and an inner restlessness that draws us further and deeper into the mystery of God. It keeps us moving on and on. This is what St Augustine referred to when he prayed: 'You have made us for yourself, O Lord, and our hearts are restless until they rest in thee.'

Our journey to God is full of mystery and variety. We are on our way with the God of surprises, the infinite, the absolute and the eternal. There are lots of experiences as we journey on. We encounter joy and sorrow, light and darkness and sometimes doubt and fear.

There are times when we feel close to God; we are aware of God's presence and feel the love all around us; we live in God's peace and walk in his light. But there are other times when it can be quite different. We may have to journey on with a deep sense of God's absence. The clouds come down and the fog surrounds us. This is the nature of the journey of faith.

And that same faith assures us that through the loving mercy of God we live and move within the circle of God's love, even when we do not feel it. We remain there, unless we fall into the most awful lack of love. The journey of faith is very much an inner journey. But it always has its outer dimensions, as we relate to others and to God's creation. Christ and his Holy Spirit are at the heart of the journey.

*Please read the following slowly and prayerfully and take time to pray for deeper faith and trust in God as you journey into the mystery, since faith opens our hearts to the mystery of God. It is like a spark that lights up our lives in such a way that God's light comes shining through in creation and in human life, even in the most ordinary events and experiences.*

*Romans 8:31-39*
*(St Paul assures us that God is always at our side on the journey)*
What then are we to say about these things? If God is for us, who is against us? He who did not withhold his own Son, but gave him up for all of us, will he not with him also give us everything else? Who will bring any charge against God's elect? It is God who justifies.

Who is to condemn? It is Christ Jesus, who died, yes, who was raised, who is at the right hand of God, who indeed intercedes for us. Who will separate us from the love of Christ? Will hardship, or distress, or persecution, or famine, or nakedness, or peril, or sword? As it is written, 'For your sake we are being killed all day long; we are accounted as sheep to be slaughtered.' No, in all these things we are more than conquerors through him who loved us. For I am convinced that neither death, nor life, nor angels, nor rulers, nor things present, nor things to come, nor powers, nor height, nor depth, nor anything else in all creation, will be able to separate us from the love of God in Christ Jesus our Lord.

*Hymn:*
*St Patrick's Breastplate,* trs Kuno Meyer
*(This hymn opens with a tremendous sense of the mystery of God.*
*There is a deep awareness of God with us on our journey, directing us*
*and guiding us with wisdom along the way, protecting us against*
*every cruel merciless power that may oppose body and soul. Notice the*
*focus on Christ.)*

I arise today,
Through the strength of heaven;
Light of sun, radiance of moon,
Splendour of fire, speed of lightning,
Swiftness of wind, depth of the sea,
Stability of earth, firmness of rock.

I arise today,
Through God's strength to pilot me.
God's eye to look before me,
God's wisdom to guide me,
God's way to lie before me,
God's shield to protect me,

From all who shall wish me ill,
Afar and anear,
Alone and in a multitude.
Against every cruel merciless power
That may oppose my body and soul.

Christ with me, Christ before me,
Christ behind me, Christ in me,
Christ beneath me, Christ above me
Christ on my right, Christ on my left.

Christ when I lie down,
Christ when I sit down, Christ when I arise,
Christ to shield me,
Christ in the heart of everyone who thinks of me,
Christ in the mouth of everyone who speaks of me.
I arise today.

## 1.6. 'The Father is fond of us'

In the introduction to his book, *The Father is Fond of Me*, Fr Edward Farrell explains how he came by the title. He was visiting Ireland many years ago and he was out walking along a country road. He met an old man and struck up a conversation with him. It started to rain and they took shelter under a tree. Soon the conversation lapsed and both were sitting there in silence, waiting for the shower to pass. Fr Farrell noticed the old man was praying. After a while, he said to him, you must be very close to God. The old man thought for a few moments and said, 'Yes, the Father is fond of me.' In a life that, no doubt, had its share of hardship and pain, the man had grown close to God. From his response we can assume that he had experienced the love of God in his heart and life.

This is the love that Jesus spoke about in St John's gospel. Jesus tells the disciples: 'The Father himself loves you, for loving me and believing that I came from God' (Jn 16:26-27). Here we have the original message of Jesus expressed in such a simple way. That sentence conveys the most profound truth at the heart of our faith.

The Father himself loves us, or, to put it in the words of the old man, the Father is fond of us.

The first letter of John expresses it in more detail: 'God showed his love for us by sending his only Son into the world, so that we might have life through him. This is what love is: it is not that we have loved God, but that he loved us and sent his Son to be our Saviour.' (1 Jn 4:9-10). This is the unique revelation that Jesus gives. As Christians, we believe not only that God loves us, but that he loves us first, and what is even more astonishing that 'God is love.'

This is the mystery that we are called to journey into as Christians by being drawn into the great stream of God's love flowing freely in our hearts and lives – 'going the heart's way.'

*Please read the following scripture passage and hymn slowly and prayerfully and remember that 'contemplative prayer is nothing else than a close sharing between friends; it means taking time frequently to be alone with him, who we know loves us' (St Teresa of Avila). Ask God the help you to experience his presence as a loving Father.*

*Luke 15:11-25*
*(The story of the prodigal son or merciful father gives us a practical illustration of how much the Father loves us. It is seldom that we find such love in our ordinary human relationships. God's way of loving is beyond our way. Yet many people come to an experience of God's love.)*

Then Jesus said, 'There was a man who had two sons. The younger of them said to his father, "Father, give me the share of the property that will belong to me." So he divided his property between them. A few days later the younger son gathered all he had and travelled to a distant country, and there he squandered his property in dissolute living. When he had spent everything, a severe famine took place throughout that country, and he began to be in need. So he went and hired himself out to one of the citizens of that country, who sent him to his fields to feed the pigs. He would gladly have filled himself with the pods that the pigs were eating; and no one gave him anything. But when he came to himself he said, "How many of my father's hired hands have bread enough and to spare, but here I am dying of hunger! I will get up and go to my father, and I will say to him, 'Father, I have sinned against heaven and before you; I am no longer worthy to be called your son; treat me like one of your hired hands'." So he set off and went to his father. But while he was still far off, his father saw him and was filled with compassion; he ran and put his arms around him and kissed him. Then the son said to him, "Father, I have sinned against heaven and before you; I am no longer worthy to be called your son." But the father said to his slaves, "Quickly, bring out a robe – the best one – and put it on him; put a ring on his finger and sandals on his feet. And get the fatted calf and kill it, and let us eat and celebrate; for this son of mine was dead and is alive again; he was lost and is found!" And they began to celebrate.'

*Psalm 71*
*(Prayer for a deep sense of God's lifelong love, protection and help)*

In you, O Lord, I take refuge;
let me never be put to shame.
In your righteousness deliver me and rescue me;
incline your ear to me and save me.
Be to me a rock of refuge,
a strong fortress to save me,
for you are my rock and my fortress.

Rescue me, O my God, from the hand of the wicked,
from the grasp of the unjust and cruel.
For you, O Lord, are my hope,
my trust, O Lord, from my youth.
Upon you I have leaned from my birth;
it was you who took me from my mother's womb.
My praise is continually of you.

My mouth is filled with your praise,
and with your glory all day long.
O God, do not be far from me;
O my God, make haste to help me!
My mouth will tell of your righteous acts,
of your deeds of salvation all day long,
though their number is past my knowledge.

O God, from my youth you have taught me,
and I still proclaim your wondrous deeds.
So even to old age and gray hairs,
O God, do not forsake me,
until I proclaim your might
to all the generations to come.
Your power and your righteousness, O God,
reach the high heavens.

## 1.7. 'God is Love'

Pope Benedict preached the homily at the funeral Mass for Pope John Paul II and again at his own installation as Pope. They were both great homilies. Yet a priest friend of mine felt that it was a missed opportunity. He felt that, with the eyes of the world on the new Pope, it was a wonderful time for him to tell the whole world about the central truth of our Catholic faith: that God loved the world so much that he sent his only Son to be our Saviour.

Then, less than a year later, came the encyclical: *God is Love*. The Pope did what my friend had hoped for, and more! The first line reads: 'God is Love and anyone who lives in love lives in God and God lives in him or her' (1 Jn 4:16). The Pope says that this text expresses with remarkable clarity the heart of the Christian faith. It gives us the Christian image of God and the resulting image of mankind and its destiny. He also notes that in the same verse, St John offers a kind of summary of the Christian life when he says: 'We have come to know and believe in the love God has for us.' And St John's gospel describes God's love in these words: 'God loved the world so much that he sent his only Begotten Son, so that everyone who believes in him may have eternal life' (Jn 3:16).

We all need to hear the message that 'God is love' and that he loves us so much. It was often missing in the past. I can remember some of the teaching and preaching about God that was popular when I was growing up. My father used to tell about a particular mission that went on in our parish. The 'missioner' gave a rousing sermon about the wrath of God and the fires of hell. He described hell in such graphic terms that you could smell the smoke and feel the heat! There was so much of that kind of thing accepted as normal at the time. If my memory serves me right, there was little reference to the love of God in the religious teaching and preaching of my early years. The fear of God and the anger of God were much more popular themes. Pope Benedict reminds us very clearly that we are children of a loving God and not of an angry God. Love flows from the heart of God, like a stream or river.

*Please read the following slowly and prayerfully and remember that 'Contemplative Prayer is a gaze of faith fixed on Jesus ... His gaze purifies our hearts; the light of his countenance illumines the eyes of our hearts and teaches us to see everything in the light of his truth and his compassion for all people' (CCC 2715). Ask God to help you to come to know and experience the healing touch of the love God has for you.*

*Luke 15:1-10*

Now all the tax collectors and sinners were coming near to listen to him. And the Pharisees and the scribes were grumbling and saying, 'This fellow welcomes sinners and eats with them.' So he told them this parable: 'Which one of you, having a hundred sheep and losing one of them, does not leave the ninety-nine in the wilderness and go after the one that is lost until he finds it? When he has found it, he lays it on his shoulders and rejoices. And when he comes home, he calls together his friends and neighbours, saying to them, "Rejoice with me, for I have found my sheep that was lost." Just so, I tell you, there will be more joy in heaven over one sinner who repents than over ninety-nine righteous persons who need no repentance. Or what woman having ten silver coins, [Gk *drachmas*, each worth about a day's wage for a labourer] if she loses one of them, does not light a lamp, sweep the house, and search carefully until she finds it? When she has found it, she calls together her friends and neighbours, saying, "Rejoice with me, for I have found the coin that I had lost."

Just so, I tell you, there is joy in the presence of the angels of God over one sinner who repents.'

*Psalms 103:1-13*
*(With the psalmist we celebrate the compassionate love of God.)*

> Bless the Lord, O my soul,
> and all that is within me,
> bless his holy name.
> Bless the Lord, O my soul,
> and do not forget all his benefits.

It is he who forgives all your iniquity,
who heals all your diseases,
who redeems your life from the pit,
who crowns you with steadfast love and mercy,
who satisfies you with good as long as you live
so that your youth is renewed like the eagle's.

The Lord is merciful and gracious,
slow to anger and abounding in steadfast love.
He does not deal with us according to our sins,
nor repay us according to our iniquities.

For as the heavens are high above the earth,
so great is his steadfast love toward those who fear him;
as far as the east is from the west,
so far he removes our transgressions from us.

PART ONE: SECTION TWO
# The Tabernacle of the Living God
## *'It is in God that we live and move and exist'*
## (Acts 17:28-29).

## 2.1. 'I myself will go with you'

The Israelites had a deep sense of God's presence with them and God's love for them. In the course of the conversation between God and Moses, Moses asks God: 'Who are you going to send with your people?' And God answers: 'I myself will go with you and I will give you rest' (Ex 33: 12-23). There is no question of sending anyone else, 'I myself will go with you' – what a powerful little expression. This work is far too important to leave to someone else; a representative will not do for such an important task. It could give the wrong impression. God himself would go with his people, to be with them, to travel with them. He would be there at all times: In the cloud by day and the fire by night (Deut 1:13).

The promise of God's presence with his people is put so simply. I sometimes wonder do we take his promise even half seriously enough. We find it in so many passages, like: 'I will never forget you, for I have carved you on the palm of my hand' (Is 49:15-16). The promise of his presence is always there – until the end of time. We no longer have the cloud by day or the fire by night but we have something infinitely better: we have God with us in Christ our Saviour.

There is also a very comforting verse in Deuteronomy that I want to refer to: 'In the wilderness, you saw how the Lord your God carried you, just as one carries a child, all along the road you have travelled on the way till you reached this place' (Deut 1:31). Here we have a God who is not only with us, but a God who carries us along the way, especially when we travel in the wilderness, where there is hardship and suffering.

This same idea is expressed in the popular poem 'Footprints'. In the version by Margaret Fishbach Powers, she describes how she had a dream that she was walking along the beach with

God. Scenes from her life flashed before her. In most of the scenes she could see two sets of 'footprints' along the beach, where they had walked. But she noticed that in certain scenes there was only one set of footprints; this seemed to happen when life was most difficult. She was surprised to find this, so she asked God why he abandoned her in those painful times, when she most needed him. God replied that he did not abandon her during those times; in fact, it was then that he carried her!

*Please read the following slowly and prayerfully. Take time. Do not rush.*

*Exodus 33:12-14*
Moses said to the Lord, 'See, you have said to me, "Bring up this people"; but you have not let me know whom you will send with me. Yet you have said, "I know you by name, and you have also found favour in my sight." Now if I have found favour in your sight, show me your ways, so that I may know you and find favour in your sight. Consider too that this nation is your people.' He said, 'My presence will go with you, and I will give you rest.'

*Psalms 16*
> Protect me, O God, for in you I take refuge.
> I say to the Lord, 'You are my Lord;
> I have no good apart from you.'

> The Lord is my chosen portion and my cup; you hold my lot.
> The boundary lines have fallen for me in pleasant places;
> I have a goodly heritage.

> I bless the Lord who gives me counsel,
> in the night also my heart instructs me.
> I keep the Lord always before me;
> because he is at my right hand, I shall not be moved.
> Therefore my heart is glad, and my soul rejoices;
> my body also rests secure.

You show me the path of life.
In your presence there is fullness of joy;
in your right hand are pleasures forevermore.

## 2.2. 'Life is the tabernacle of the living God'

God loves us before we love him. God calls on us before we call
on God. We always have the promise of his presence. God is always near us, with us and in us. But we are often like the little
fish, swimming around in the great ocean. Someone had told the
fish how great the ocean was. The fish was swimming around
looking for the ocean, not realising that it was all the time swimming in the ocean. We too are living in the presence of God,
often not realising it.

Joan Chittister uses helpful images to describe the mystery of
God, in whom we live and move and have our being. The
Christian 'lives and breathes in the womb of God'. And later she
writes that every day the Christian 'makes a new beginning, trying to plumb the meaning of life; every day the Christian disap-
pears again into the heart of God, so present in us and in the
world around us, if we only realise it'.

One last little gem of a phrase: 'Faith is about knowing that
life is the tabernacle of the living God.'[3] We can add that each
person is a tabernacle of the living God.

St Ignatius described this in terms of finding God in all things.
He encouraged his followers 'to practise the seeking of God's
presence in all things: in their conversations, their walks, in all
they see, taste, hear, understand, and in all their actions – since
The Divine Majesty is truly in all things by his presence, and
power.' Thus in the Jesuit approach to life, a person is encouraged
to cultivate the habit of reviewing the experiences and events of
the day in order to 'notice' or 'discern' the presence of God.

By doing this, our relationship with God is solidly anchored
in the ordinary events and experiences of life. It is very important to notice what we experience and what is happening before
our eyes. There are so many acts of kindness and love that we do
not notice. Perhaps we need to train ourselves to be more aware
of the goodness that shines through the simplest events and experiences in our lives.

---

3. Joan Chittister, *Illuminated Life: Monastic Wisdom for Seekers of Light,*
Orbis, 2000, pages 19 and 38.

*Please read the following slowly and prayerfully and remember that 'Contemplative Prayer is a gaze of faith fixed on Jesus … His gaze purifies our hearts; the light of his countenance illumines the eyes of our hearts and teaches us to see everything in the light of his truth and his compassion for all people' (CCC 2715). Ask God to help you to feel and experience the healing touch of his loving presence.*

*Isaiah 43:1-5*

But now thus says the Lord, he who created you, O Jacob, he who formed you, O Israel: Do not fear, for I have redeemed you; I have called you by name, you are mine. When you pass through the waters, I will be with you; and through the rivers, they shall not overwhelm you; when you walk through fire you shall not be burned, and the flame shall not consume you. For I am the Lord your God, the Holy One of Israel, your Saviour. I give Egypt as your ransom, Ethiopia; Heb and Seba in exchange for you. Because you are precious in my sight, and honoured, and I love you, I give people in return for you, nations in exchange for your life. Do not fear, for I am with you.

*Psalms 91*
*(Assurance of God's Presence and Protection in the midst of life)*

You who live in the shelter of the Most High,
who abide in the shadow of the Almighty,
will say to the Lord, 'My refuge and my fortress;
my God, in whom I trust.'

For he will deliver you from the snare of the fowler
and from the deadly pestilence;
he will cover you with his pinions,
and under his wings you will find refuge;
his faithfulness is a shield and buckler.

You will not fear the terror of the night,
or the arrow that flies by day,
or the pestilence that stalks in darkness,
or the destruction that wastes at noonday.

Because you have made the Lord your refuge,
the Most High your dwelling place,
no evil shall befall you,
no scourge come near your tent.

For he will command his angels concerning you
to guard you in all your ways.
On their hands they will bear you up,
so that you will not dash your foot against a stone.

Those who love me, I will deliver;
I will protect those who know my name.
When they call to me, I will answer them;
I will be with them in trouble,
I will rescue them and honour them.
With long life I will satisfy them,
and show them my salvation. Amen.

## 2.3. 'You were with me but I was not with you'

In a well-known passage from the *Confessions* of St Augustine (given below), we find powerful images expressing Augustine's sense of God trying to get through to him, and how he discovered that he himself was a tabernacle of the living God. From his experience of conversion,[4] he concluded that God was always with him but he was not with God: 'You were with me but I was not with you … You were within me, while I was outside.' We can reflect on the images used; all five senses are involved in his deep personal experience: God shattered his deafness; God put his blindness to flight; God sent forth fragrance; he got a taste of God and he experienced a hunger and thirst for God; he felt the touch of God and burned for his peace.

Augustine actually felt that he was fenced in on all sides by God. He was left with a profound sense that God was loving him all his life, searching for him and calling to him: 'You urged me on … so that from afar I would hear you and be converted, and call upon you, as you called to me.'

Augustine found the idea of God's search summed up in the simple question that God asks in the Garden of Eden: Adam where are you? (Gen 3:9). This question took on great significance for Augustine; he felt that God was saying the same thing to him: Augustine where are you? And indeed, he decided that this is the question which everyone has to answer: where are you in the journey of life? Where are you spiritually? Where are you in your relationship with God? Ultimately, there is no hiding place; there is no escaping God. He searches for us; He loves us and he knows us inside out. God is within and we are often outside.

*Please read the following slowly and prayerfully and ask God to help you to feel his touch, to hear his call, to see his light, to taste his presence and to hunger and thirst for his love.*

---

4. You will find the story of his conversion in *The Confessions of Saint Augustine*, trs John K Ryan, Image Books, 1960, Book VIII, chapter 8 to 12. and in Bk. X, 38 – passage 'Too Late I have …'

From *The Confessions of St Augustine – The Everlasting Love*
'Too late I have loved you, O beauty so ancient and so new, too
late have I loved you! Behold, you were within me, while I was
outside: It was there that I sought you and, a deformed creature,
rushed headlong upon these things of beauty, which you have
made. You were with me, but I was not with you. They kept me
far from you, those fair things which, if they were not in you,
would not exist at all. You have called to me, and have cried out,
and have sheltered my deafness. You have blazed forth with
light, and have shone upon me, and you have put my blindness
to flight! You have sent forth fragrance, and I have drawn in my
breath, and I pant after you. I have tasted you, and I hunger and
thirst after you. You have touched me, and I have burned for
your peace.'

*Psalms 63 (Thirsting for God's loving presence)*
    O God, you are my God, I seek you,
      my soul thirsts for you; my flesh faints for you,
      as in a dry and weary land where there is no water.
    So I have looked upon you in the sanctuary,
    Beholding your power and glory.

    Because your steadfast love is better than life,
    my lips will praise you.
    So I will bless you as long as I live;
    I will lift up my hands and call on your name.
    My soul is satisfied as with a rich feast,
    and my mouth praises you with joyful lips

    When I think of you on my bed,
    and meditate on you in the watches of the night;
    for you have been my help,
    and in the shadow of your wings I sing for joy.
    My soul clings to you; your right hand upholds me.

## 2.4. 'The kingdom of God is here'

To help us experience life as the Tabernacle of God, we need to reflect on an image that is central to the teaching of Jesus, namely, the kingdom of God. It is more than an image; it is a reality and an experience that we are drawn into as we feel our way towards God. The 'kingdom' may not be among your favourite words but the 'kingdom of God' is the expression used to translate one of the key concepts in the original message of Jesus. In his very first words, as recorded in St Mark's gospel, He announces that the kingdom is here (Mk 1:14-15). In that same verse of scripture we find the call to repentance (conversion).

We note here that the good news about the kingdom of God being here is the first part of the message. Fortunately, there is widespread agreement among scripture scholars about the meaning of this expression in the context in which Jesus was using it. We can sum it up in this way: The kingdom of God refers to the mystery of God's saving presence, power and love being made manifest in our hearts, in our lives, and in our world – renewing and reconciling all things. It is both a process (the reign of God) and a reality towards which the process is moving (the kingdom of God). It happens in Christ and through his Holy Spirit.

We can get good insights into the nature of the kingdom if we take time to reflect on the parables about the kingdom. We begin with the man who sells all to buy the field where he has found the treasure. And in that same short passage from St Matthew we find the merchant selling everything to buy the fine pearl, which he found. This is what the kingdom of God is like. We are advised to be concerned above everything else with the kingdom of God and with what God requires of us (Mt 6:33). Ask God to help you to feel and experience the healing touch of his saving power and loving presence – his kingdom, and to be able to respond generously.

*Please read the following slowly and prayerfully. You may want to read them a second time. Then you can pick out some of the verses or phrases that have touched you deeply. Let them sink into your heart and being. Take time. Do not rush.*

*Matthew 13:44-50*

The kingdom of heaven is like treasure hidden in a field, which someone found and hid; then in his joy he goes and sells all that he has and buys that field. Again, the kingdom of heaven is like a merchant in search of fine pearls; on finding one pearl of great value, he went and sold all that he had and bought it.

*Psalm 145: 1-9*
*(Celebrating the greatness and goodness of God's kingdom)*

I will extol you, my God and King,
and bless your name forever and ever.
Every day I will bless you,
and praise your name forever and ever.

Great is the Lord and greatly to be praised;
his greatness is unsearchable.
On the glorious splendour of your majesty
and of your works, I will meditate.

The might of your awesome deeds will be proclaimed,
and I will declare your greatness.

The Lord is gracious and merciful,
slow to anger and abounding in selfless love.
The Lord is good to all
and his compassion is over all that he has made.

My mouth will speak the praise of the Lord,
and all flesh will bless his Holy Name forever and ever. Amen.

## 2.5. The seed grows in silence

The seed of God's kingdom is growing constantly in our hearts and lives. This is the mystery of the kingdom of God (Mk. 4:26-31). This is what Christ teaches us in his parables about the kingdom. Jesus tells us: the kingdom of God is here; the kingdom of God is among us; the kingdom of God is in us. Thus each of us is a tabernacle of the living God.

Jesus points us to the world of nature, where we can get some deep insights into the mystery of the kingdom of God – the mystery of God's loving presence in our hearts, in our lives and in all of creation. There we find the mystery of God's power at work in the world before our very eyes; change, growth and transformation are taking place, night and day, while we sleep, while we are awake – how we do not know. There we can see the cycle of life, death, and new life: the seed falls on the ground and dies and produces fruit a hundredfold. God's saving power is being made manifest in all of creation. It is that same power and love that is flowing constantly in our hearts. And it can produce infinitely more than we can ask or imagine (Eph 3:21). It all happens in silence, almost secretly; the seed grows in silence; the flower opens in silence; God dwells in silence; his love flows in silence. It is in silence that his embrace is most keenly felt – an embrace that draws us right into the heart of God – the heart of his kingdom.

In *The Merchant of Venice* Portia says: 'How far that little candle throws its beams. So shines a good deed in a naughty world.' The saving power and love of God (the kingdom) often needs only a tiny window to make itself manifest in our hearts, lives and world. And this seems to be the way God works. Otherwise we might misunderstand his power and feel we can control it.

*Please read the following slowly and prayerfully and pray for the embrace of God that draws you right into the heart of his kingdom*

*Mark 4:26-32*

He also said, 'The kingdom of God is as if someone would scatter seed on the ground, and would sleep and rise night and day, and the seed would sprout and grow, he does not know how.' He also said, 'With what can we compare the kingdom of God, or what parable will we use for it? It is like a mustard seed, which, when sown upon the ground, is the smallest of all the seeds on earth; yet when it is sown it grows up and becomes the greatest of all shrubs, and puts forth large branches, so that the birds of the air can make nests in its shade.'

*Psalms 145:9-21*
*(Celebrating God's kingdom of graciousness and compassion)*

The Lord is good to all,
and his compassion is over all that he has made.
All your works shall give thanks to you, O Lord,
and all your faithful shall bless you.

They shall speak of the glory of your kingdom,
and tell of your power,
to make known to all people your mighty deeds,
and the glorious splendour of your kingdom.

Your kingdom is an everlasting kingdom,
and your dominion endures throughout all generations.
The Lord is faithful in all his words,
and gracious in all his deeds.
The Lord upholds all who are falling,
and raises up all who are bowed down.

The eyes of all look to you,
and you give them their food in due season.
You open your hand,
Satisfying the desire of every living thing.

## 2.6. The kingdom of God – An Experience

We can continue to reflect on the kingdom and what it teaches us about human life and about each person being a tabernacle of the living God. The kingdom reaches deep into our human hearts and human experience.

According to the parables in Matthew, the kingdom is like the tiny seed growing, the leaven working in the lump of dough, the treasure hidden in a field, which is there to be found by those who know its worth. The kingdom of God is like the pearl of great price, which can be purchased by those who recognise its value. The kingdom of God is an image, a symbol, a concept and an experience; it is not a place; neither is it an abstract concept. It is rather an experience that comes through faith – it is an experience of God's saving power and God's loving presence. We begin to taste it in an experience of being at peace with God, with oneself, with others and with creation.

There are various words used to describe this kind of experience: mystical, spiritual, religious experience, or, coming from the angle of psychology – a peak or depth experience. It is the experience that is at the heart of Christian faith, Christian life, Christian conversion and Christian mission. The form it takes varies from person to person – it can be a Damascus road experience, as St Paul had, or it can just be the slow maturing process of a lifetime of prayer, love and service.

The experience of God can be a positive, joyful experience or it can take place in some dark moments, as Brian Keenan the journalist experienced. He was held in captivity in Beirut for five years by Muslim extremists. He wrote: 'At times God seemed so real and so intimately close. We talked [himself and his companion, John McCarthy] not of a God in the Christian tradition but of some force more primitive, more immediate, and more vital, a presence rather than a set of beliefs … In its own way our isolation had expanded the heart not to reach out to a detached God, but to find and become part of whatever God may be.'[5]

---

5. Brian Keenan, *An Evil Cradling*, Vintage, 1992, p 99.

*Please read the following slowly and prayerfully and pray for the embrace of God that draws you right into the heart of his kingdom*

*Romans 14:17*
For the kingdom of God is not food and drink but righteousness and peace and joy in the Holy Spirit.

*Matthew 13:33*
He told them another parable: 'The kingdom of heaven is like yeast that a woman took and mixed in with three measures of flour until all of it was leavened.'

Hymn:
(*St Patrick's Breastplate*, trs Kuno Meyer)
(*We have used this hymn already. I repeat it here because it opens us to a tremendous sense of the mystery of God's kingdom. We can experience the presence of God (his kingdom) in the world of nature, in the midst of human life and in the depths of the human heart. The hymn also places Christ at the centre of our experience of God's kingdom.*)

> I arise today,
> Through the strength of heaven;
> Light of sun, radiance of moon,
> Splendour of fire, speed of lightning,
> Swiftness of wind, depth of the sea,
> Stability of earth, firmness of rock.
>
> I arise today,
> Through God's strength to pilot me.
> God's eye to look before me,
> God's wisdom to guide me,
> God's way to lie before me,
> God's shield to protect me,
>
> From all who shall wish me ill,
> Afar and anear,
> Alone and in a multitude.
> Against every cruel merciless power
> That may oppose my body and soul.

Christ with me, Christ before me,
Christ behind me, Christ in me,
Christ beneath me, Christ above me
Christ on my right, Christ on my left.

Christ when I lie down,
Christ when I sit down, Christ when I arise,
 Christ to shield me,
Christ in the heart of everyone who thinks of me,
Christ in the mouth of everyone who speaks of me.
I arise today.

## 2.7. An awakened heart

The image of 'awakening' is useful to describe our way into the experience of life as a tabernacle of the living God. We 'wake up' to the reality of God in the midst of life. The contrast between being asleep and being awake expresses rather well the change that comes about. The person wakes up to the presence of God's love and forgiveness. And the more we realise that life is the tabernacle of God, the more we will be in touch with the reality of sin or sinfulness. We see this in the lives of the saints; genuinely holy people have a deep sense of God's love and a profound awareness of their own sinfulness; they are shocked and appalled at the reality of sin, but always full of trust in God's goodness. There are no illusions about being saved, holy, a saint. St Augustine felt he was both a saint and a sinner all his life; there were weeds among the wheat until the day he died.

Nobody has the experience of being utterly pure and holy in this life. The purest, the best, and the holiest are very much aware of this; they are in touch with their brokenness, their faults and failings. In the great saints you will find a profound awareness of their sinfulness and a deep trust in God's love; this brings a sense of hope. Julian of Norwich is a good example: she wrote about visions that she had in her *Showings of Divine Love*. She saw Christ holding a globe (representing the universe) in a loving embrace, and she describes her feeling of hope in the well-known phrase: 'All will be well – all manner of thing will be well.'

*Please read the following slowly and prayerfully and pray for the grace to wake up to the reality of God's forgiveness and your own sinfulness.*

*John 8:3-11*
*(In this story, Jesus very cleverly makes each person focus on their own sinfulness and then reveals his compassion for the woman.)*

The scribes and the Pharisees brought a woman who had been caught in adultery; and making her stand before all of them, they said to him, 'Teacher, this woman was caught in the very act of committing adultery. Now in the law, Moses commanded us to stone such women. Now what do you say?' They said this to test him, so that they might have some charge to bring against him. Jesus bent down and wrote with his finger on the ground. When they kept on questioning him, he straightened up and said to them, 'Let anyone among you who is without sin be the first to throw a stone at her.' And once again he bent down and wrote on the ground. When they heard it, they went away, one by one, beginning with the elders; and Jesus was left alone with the woman standing before him. Jesus straightened up and said to her, 'Woman, where are they? Has no one condemned you?' She said, 'No one, sir.' And Jesus said, 'Neither do I condemn you. Go your way, and from now on do not sin again.'

*Psalm 57*
*(The heart and soul awakening to God's love and protection)*

> Be merciful to me, O God, be merciful to me,
> for in you my soul takes refuge;
> in the shadow of your wings I will take refuge,
> until the destroying storms pass by.
>
> I cry to God Most High,
> to God who fulfills his purpose for me.
> He will send from heaven and save me,
> he will put to shame those who trample on me.
> God will send forth his steadfast love and his faithfulness.
>
> My heart is steadfast, O God,
> my heart is steadfast.
> I will sing and make melody.
> Awake, my soul!
> Awake, O harp and lyre!
> I will awake the dawn.

I will give thanks to you, O Lord, among the peoples;
I will sing praises to you among the nations.
For your steadfast love is as high as the heavens;
your faithfulness extends to the clouds.
Be exalted, O God, above the heavens.
Let your glory be over all the earth.

PART ONE: SECTION THREE
# Going the Heart's Way
*As we open our hearts to God-with-us in Christ*

## 3.1. Opening our hearts to 'God-with-us' in Christ

The affective, experiential area of life is central, as we open our hearts to the mystery of God. We have 'to go the heart's way' and let ourselves be loved by getting a deep sense of God's loving presence with us in Christ and his Spirit. We have to take the Incarnation seriously. God's love is revealed in the wonder of the Incarnation. Christ is God-with-us. We need to pray for the grace to open our hearts to Christ, so that we can know him better, love him more and serve him faithfully. In this way we can deepen our love for him and experience a deep friendship with him.

The readings for the feast of Christmas can help us here. At Midnight Mass, we celebrate the birth of a child who was to bring the joy of God's saving love to all people. Christ is Emmanuel, a name which means 'God is with us.' Christ is the human face of God. In Christ we meet God face to face. Through Christ and his Spirit we can come to know God and experience his presence and love. What a blessing it is if we feel we know God. Here our English word 'knowledge' is a weak word to translate the original word, which refers more to what we might call 'experience' and 'feeling' – located in the area of the heart. What is being referred to is a kind of experiential knowledge of God, of 'the loving kindness of the heart of our God, who visits us like the dawn from the high' (*Benedictus*). This is what is open to us through the gift of our faith. We can have the experience of letting ourselves be loved by God. 'This is what God wants for us: the whole meaning of our existence and the one consuming desire of the heart of God is that we let ourselves be loved' (*Ruth Burrows*).

We ask God to help us to truly experience the presence and love of Christ in our hearts and in all the events and experiences of life and in the hearts and culture of people everywhere. This is what we call 'going the heart's way.'

*Scripture*
*We need to spend much time reflecting on the wonder of the Incarnation and on the simple phrases that are so familiar to us:*
– The Word was made flesh and dwells among us (Jn 1:14);
– Jesus is Emmanuel, a name which means God is with us (Mt 1:23);
– Jesus is the radiant light of God's glory and the perfect copy of his nature (Heb 1:3);
– All the ends of the earth have seen the saving power of our God (Is 52:10).
– The message of the angel to the shepherds: Do not be afraid, Listen, I bring you news of great joy, a joy to be shared by the whole people. Today in the town of David a Saviour has been born to you. He is Christ the Lord (Lk 2:10-11).

*Hymn*
*(This is an extract from the hymn* Visions, *already used in Reflection 1.2. In this extract the focus is on the Incarnation and the Eucharist – notice the images used.)*

The love of the Father took flesh in the Son;
The love of the Son still lives in his friends;
The love of the Spirit is born in each heart,
Awaiting, awakening when rocks break apart.

Lord Jesus Christ, my King, my Sun,
You are the source whence love's rays come;
You shine through all things, your loving flows.
Through bread and wine, your presence grows.

I sense your light in every ray;
I see you shape each break of day;
In Bread and Wine though our eyes can't see,
I sense your love enliven me.

I see your rays one with the sun;
I see them reach to everyone;
In Bread and Wine Lord remembered be;
transform our lives, Lord make us free.

## 3.2. The heart of our God revealed in Christ

When I was growing up every home had a large picture of the Sacred Heart of Jesus. The picture usually hung on the wall of the kitchen. This was the big room at the centre of the house – so much happened there. All the cooking was done in that room, but it also functioned as the dining room and sitting room. In the winter it was the only warm room in the house. The big open fire was constantly blazing. The kitchen was a hive of activity from early morning until late into the night. People, young and old, were constantly coming and going. There were no formalities. It was the centre of hospitality. I have great memories of the warmth and friendship experienced in the kitchen. Presiding over all that happened there was the big picture of the Sacred Heart. It may not meet the requirements of the art critics, but it conveyed a powerful message to one and all. It symbolised the love of God for each one of us, as it is revealed and communicated through the heart of Jesus.

The 'heart' is the universal symbol of love. This word is found in many languages, cultures and faiths. It points to the centre of the personality, where we find the source of life, love, and knowledge. It signifies the disposition and the attitude with which a person lives and looks at other people, at life and at all that exist. Sometimes the word has been abused, but it retains its real significance for most people. We are told that the word 'heart' occurs around a thousand times in the Bible. According to McKenzie's *Dictionary of the Bible* the word 'heart' means even more in Hebrew than it does in English. In Hebrew thought it signifies the entire inner life of a person. And it is normally used in this figurative sense. This gives us further insights into what it means 'to go the heart's way'.

The word 'heart' is applied to God many times in expressions such as: 'The loving kindness of the heart of our God, visits us like the dawn from on high.' We can reflect on the heart of God and on the sacred heart of Jesus, who is God-with-us. What a powerful symbol to convey the message of God's infinite love and mercy for all mankind.

*Please read the following slowly and carefully and ask God to help you to experience his infinite love for all mankind as it pours our from his heart day and night, while we sleep, while we are awake, how we do not know.*

Matthew 15:32-39
*(In this text from Matthew Jesus refers to his own heart. Some commentators tell us that the better translation of the opening verse 32 is: 'My heart goes out to all these people.' This verse conveys briefly but very movingly the compassion of Jesus for the suffering crowds.)*
Then Jesus called his disciples to him and said, 'I have compassion for the crowd, because they have been with me now for three days and have nothing to eat; and I do not want to send them away hungry, for they might faint on the way.' The disciples said to him, 'Where are we to get enough bread in the desert to feed so great a crowd?' Jesus asked them, 'How many loaves have you?' They said, 'Seven, and a few small fish.' Then ordering the crowd to sit down on the ground, he took the seven loaves and the fish; and after giving thanks he broke them and gave them to the disciples, and the disciples gave them to the crowds. And all of them ate and were filled; and they took up the broken pieces left over, seven baskets full. Those who had eaten were four thousand men, besides women and children.

*Hymn*

> The Father's glory, Christ our light,
> With love and mercy comes to span
> The vast abyss of sin between
> The God of holiness and man.
>
> Christ yesterday and Christ today,
> For all eternity the same,
> The image of our hidden God;
> Eternal Wisdom is his name.
> He keeps his word from age to age,
> Is with us to the end of days,

A cloud by day, a flame by night,
To go before us on his ways.

We bless you, Father, fount of light,
And Christ, your well-beloved Son,
Who with the Spirit dwell in us:
Immortal Trinity in one.
*(Stanbrook Abbey)*

## 3.3. The Sacred Heart of Jesus

Like so many of their generation my parents had great devotion to the Sacred Heart. I am convinced that it opened up a whole world for them, in which they came to know and experience the love and mercy of God. It compensated in many ways for the preaching and teaching of that time, which was more likely to focus on the fear of God and even the anger of God.

The importance of this devotion was brought home to me when my father was dying of cancer. He was in the Bon Secour hospital in Tralee for nearly two months. It was a slow death, with its share of suffering, yet he remained remarkably peaceful most of the time. One evening when I was at his bedside, shortly before he died, we got talking about his suffering, and in the course of our conversation he pointed to a big picture of the Sacred Heart on the wall of the public ward he was in. Then he said 'I keep my eyes on that picture, and keep saying: Sacred Heart of Jesus I place my trust in thee, and I feel the Lord's presence with me. It is a great help to me.' That made me realise how deep the devotion to the Sacred Heart could be. For many people, it was a way into the heart of Jesus, into the very heart of God. They were truly 'going the heart's way'.

Pope John Paul II reflected on the Sacred Heart of Jesus when he visited the Basilica of the Sacred Heart at Montmartre, in Paris: 'We are in the evening of the first of June, the day of the month particularly dedicated to meditation, to contemplation of Christ's love manifested by his Sacred Heart. Here, day and night, Christians gather in succession to seek "the unsearchable riches of Christ" (cf Eph 3:8). We are called not only to meditate on and contemplate this mystery of Christ's love. We are called to take part in it. It is the mystery of the Holy Eucharist, the centre of our worship of Christ's merciful love manifested in his Sacred Heart, a mystery which is adored here night and day, in this basilica … We come here to contemplate the love of the Lord Jesus: his compassionate kindness to everyone during his earthly life; his predilection for children, the sick, the afflicted. Let us contemplate his infinite love, that of the eternal Son, who leads us to the very mystery of God.'

*Please read the following scripture passage and hymn slowly and prayerfully. You may want to read them more than once. Then you can pick out some of the verses or phrases that have touched you deeply. Let them sink into your heart and being. Take time.*

Luke 23: 32-38
*(The stories about Jesus on the cross manifest the deep emotion and compassion of the heart of Jesus in the midst of his anguish. In this story, we have to be struck by the fact that his final words on the cross are words of mercy and forgiveness. This has deep significance for all who believe in the forgiving love of Christ.)*

Two others also, who were criminals, were led away to be put to death with him. When they came to the place that is called The Skull, they crucified Jesus there with the criminals, one on his right and one on his left. Then Jesus said, 'Father, forgive them; for they do not know what they are doing.' And they cast lots to divide his clothing. And the people stood by, watching; but the leaders scoffed at him, saying, 'He saved others; let him save himself if he is the Messiah of God, his chosen one!' The soldiers also mocked him, coming up and offering him sour wine and saying, 'If you are the King of the Jews, save yourself!' There was also an inscription over him: 'This is the King of the Jews.'

*Hymn*

> The love of God was shown to man,
> in Christ our Saviour's wounded heart;
> He asks us now to take his cross.
> And in his passion take our part.
>
> We are the Father's gift to Christ,
> who loves his own until the end,
> whose burden light we bear with joy,
> and gladly to his yoke we bend.
>
> Where love and loving-kindness are,
> the God of love will always be;

he binds us with a weightless chain,
that leaves the willing captive free.

Praise father, Son and Spirit blest,
Eternal Trinity sublime,
who make their home in humble hearts,
indwelling to the end of time.
*(Stanbrook Abbey Hymnal)*

## 3.4. 'I am gentle and humble in heart' (Mt 11:28-30)

This verse of scripture (Mt 11:28) has to be one of the most beautiful and comforting verses in the New Testament. It is one of the few passages where Jesus refers to his own heart. He uses this wonderful symbol to convey the gentleness and humility with which he greets us when we come to him, especially when we are struggling and feel down beneath our burdens, when our hearts are troubled and our souls are weary.

A few years ago a man I knew well committed suicide. He had been in the depths of depression for some time. We were all in a state of shock and total bewilderment. His family, friends and neighbours were devastated. I shall never forget the pain and anguish of his family members as they gathered round the coffin to say their last farewells.

In the church, on the evening of the removal, the priest read this short verse of scripture from Matthew. Then using the man's name he repeated it. '… come to me, you who labour and are over burdened, and I will give you rest … learn from me, for I am gentle and humble of heart, and you will find rest for your soul.'

This was a most powerful, moving moment. All present drew some comfort from this verse of scripture. It assured us all that the one we had known and loved was at rest and at peace and had been freed from being over-burdened. He had gone home to his Lord, whose love and warmth was symbolised by the gentle, humble heart of Christ our Saviour. A family member said to me later that those words of scripture threw some light on what had happened and gave great comfort at the time.

*Please read the following slowly and prayerfully and ask Christ to reveal himself to you, with all the love of his gentle and humble heart. Take time. Do not rush.*

*Matthew 11:28-30*
'Come to me, all you that are weary and are carrying heavy burdens, and I will give you rest. Take my yoke upon you, and learn

from me; for I am gentle and humble in heart, and you will find rest for your souls. For my yoke is easy, and my burden is light.'

*John 11:28-37*
*(This passage from John stands out as a wonderful manifestation of the deep emotion and love of Christ's heart.)*

Martha went back and called her sister Mary, and told her privately, 'The Teacher is here and is calling for you.' And when she heard it, she got up quickly and went to him. Now Jesus had not yet come to the village, but was still at the place where Martha had met him. The Jews who were with her in the house, consoling her, saw Mary get up quickly and go out. They followed her because they thought that she was going to the tomb to weep there. When Mary came where Jesus was and saw him, she knelt at his feet and said to him, 'Lord, if you had been here, my brother would not have died.' When Jesus saw her weeping, and the Jews who came with her also weeping, he was greatly disturbed in spirit and deeply moved. He said, 'Where have you laid him?' They said to him, 'Lord, come and see.' Jesus began to weep. So the Jews said, 'See how he loved him!'

*Psalms 131*
*(Quiet trust of a humble heart)*

> O Lord, my heart is not proud,
> my eyes are not raised too high;
> I do not occupy myself with things too great
> and too marvellous for me.
> But I have calmed and quieted my soul,
> like a weaned child with its mother;
> my soul within me is like a weaned child.
>
> O Israel, hope in the Lord
> from this time on and forevermore.

## 3.5. Love beyond all telling – on lonely roads

There is nothing soft or sentimental about the love that is symbolised by the Sacred Heart of Jesus. It is a love that was and is always gentle and humble, but it is a love that is passionate and intense. It is a love that led Jesus all the way to the anguish of Gethsemane and to death on Calvary. This love of Christ is still being made manifest in the lives of Christians today. They 'go the heart's way' with courage and commitment. There are many who witness to Christ's love in daily living, sometimes with great heroism, as they struggle to cope with suffering and problems in life. Then there are a few who are led by that same love to suffer and even to die for others in our troubled world.

Every year between twenty and thirty Catholic missionaries are murdered, most of them brutally killed for speaking out about injustice and the abuse of human rights. Two of our Mill Hill Missionaries are counted among those who died in recent years. Fr Declan O'Toole from Headford, County Galway, was murdered in Northern Uganda on 21 March 2002. And Fr John Kaiser from the United States was murdered in Kenya on 24 August 2000. They died on lonely roads far from their families and far from their homes. Declan was only thirty-one. John was sixty-four. They were both brutally murdered – martyrs for justice and the rights of innocent people.

The deaths of Declan and John (and all the others) bring home to us what love in the name of Jesus is all about. There is one side of loving that is gentle and humble, as it is lived out in loving others in ordinary daily living. But there is another side to Christian love that takes us deep into compassion, which really means to journey with others in their suffering. This can bring pain and anguish. It demands great courage and generosity of spirit. Sometimes it can lead people into very dangerous situations in certain parts of the world. Occasionally, it can and does lead to the ultimate sacrifice of giving one's life, with a love that is deep and passionate. John and Declan (and all the others) are martyrs of our time. Their hearts were engaged with suffering humanity. They 'went the heart's way' to the point of death.

*Please read the following slowly and prayerfully and ask God to help you to experience the love of the gentle and humble heart of Christ in all its passion and intensity.*

## 1 John 3:16

This has taught us love – that he gave up his life for us; and we too ought to give up our lives for our brothers and sisters.

## Luke 23: 33-46 (NJB)

*(Pray that you will come to know the amazing love and compassion that flows from the heart of Christ in the midst of his anguish – as he asked for pardon for his executioners and promised paradise to the good thief before he said: 'Father into your hands I commend my spirit.')*

It was now about noon, and darkness came over the whole land [or earth] until three in the afternoon, while the sun's light failed; [or the sun was eclipsed or the sun was darkened] and the curtain of the temple was torn in two. Then Jesus, crying with a loud voice, said, 'Father, into your hands I commend my spirit.' Having said this, he breathed his last. When the centurion saw what had taken place, he praised God and said, 'Certainly this man was innocent.' And when all the crowds who had gathered there for this spectacle saw what had taken place, they returned home, beating their breasts. But all his acquaintances, including the women who had followed him from Galilee, stood at a distance, watching these things.

## The Benedictus (Lk 1:68-79)

*(That we might serve the Lord without fear, in holiness and righteousness all our days)*

Blessed be the Lord, the God of Israel,
for he has looked favourably on his people and redeemed them.
He has raised up a mighty saviour for us
in the house of his servant David,
as he spoke through the mouth of his holy prophets from of old,
that we would be saved from our enemies and from the hand of
all who hate us.

Thus he has shown the mercy promised to our ancestors,
and has remembered his holy covenant,
the oath that he swore to our ancestor Abraham,
to grant us that we, being rescued from the hands of our enemies,
might serve him without fear, in holiness and righteousness
before him all our days.

And you, little child, will be called the prophet of the Most High;
for you will go before the Lord to prepare his ways,
to give knowledge of salvation to his people
by the forgiveness of their sins.

By the tender mercy of our God,
the dawn from on high will break upon us,
to give light to those who sit in darkness and in the shadow of
death,
to guide our feet into the way of peace.

## 3.6. Journey through life with Christ

Christ invites us to live with him – with love, peace and even joy in our hearts and lives. This is what 'going the heart's way' is about.

Christ is with us in the midst of life, often in our confused and wounded state, scarred and affected by our own sins and the sins of others on life's journey. We can find ourselves locked into negative, destructive habits or, as somebody put it, stuck in the barbed wire – desperately wanting to free ourselves but finding it difficult to do so. And indeed it does not get any easier as we get older. Yet, it is never too late to change or go on changing; as Cardinal Newman said: 'To live is to change and to be perfect is to have changed often.'

Christ is with us in our struggles, in our experience of weakness and limitations; they can be a huge burden to bear but they can also be the source of many blessings. They help to keep us humble and to make us aware of our total dependence on God: 'I am most happy, then, to be proud of my weaknesses, in order to feel the protection of Christ's power over me' (2 Cor 12:9b). With the eyes of faith we can recognise Christ's presence with us in our struggles and our suffering. Sometimes this recognition only happens later.

Christ is with us in our sinful state – as Zachaeus and so many others discover. St Paul reminds us that Jesus died for us while we were still sinners. He comes to us and loves us as we are. He invites us to repent, to change and gives us the strength to do so, through the experience of his love and forgiveness. We cannot set limits to his mercy. A change of heart is always possible as long as we allow him to love us. St Augustine pictures the Spirit of God hovering 'in love over the fragments of our brokenness; over the dark and storm-tossed waters, God hovers in mercy.' St Teresa of Avila looked upon her faults and failings as an opportunity to jump into the arms of her Saviour.

*Please read the following slowly and prayerfully. Take time. Do not rush.*

*John 8:1-11*

Early in the morning Jesus came again to the temple. All the people came to him and he sat down and began to teach them. The scribes and the Pharisees brought a woman who had been caught in adultery; and making her stand before all of them, they said to him, 'Teacher, this woman was caught in the very act of committing adultery. Now in the law Moses commanded us to stone such women. Now what do you say?' They said this to test him, so that they might have some charge to bring against him. Jesus bent down and wrote with his finger on the ground. When they kept on questioning him, he straightened up and said to them, 'Let anyone among you who is without sin be the first to throw a stone at her.' And once again he bent down and wrote on the ground. When they heard this, they went away, one by one, beginning with the elders; and Jesus was left alone with the woman standing before him. Jesus straightened up and said to her, 'Woman, where are they? Has no one condemned you?' She said, 'No one, sir.' And Jesus said, 'Neither do I condemn you. Go your way, and from now on do not sin again.'

*Hymn*

> We bless you, Father, Lord of life,
> To whom all living things tend,
> The source of holiness and grace,
> Our first beginning and our end.
>
> We give you thanks, Redeeming Christ,
> Who bore our weight of sin and shame;
> In dark defeat you conquered sin,
> And death by dying, overcame.

Come, Holy Spirit, searching fire,
Whose flame all evil burns away.
Come down to us with light and love,
In silence and in peace to stay.

We praise you, Trinity in One,
Sublime in majesty and might,
Who reign for ever, Lord of all,
In splendour and unending light.
(*Stanbrook Abbey Hymnal*)

## 3.7. 'Going the heart's way' with Christ

We can go further in the way we understand Christ's presence with us, when we discover the interior nature of that presence. St Paul tells us that Christ lives in our hearts through faith (Eph 3:16), and that our hearts are God's temple (2 Cor 6:16). Here we have deep insights into 'going the heart's way.'

We find more in Galatians Chapter 1 and 2, where we get a glimpse of the infinite depth that St Paul sees in the mystery of Christ's presence in our hearts. Paul writes: 'God ... called me through his grace and chose to reveal his Son in me' or 'He chose to uncover his Son in me.' In this verse we see how Paul experienced and viewed his encounter with Christ. This was Paul's personal experience of Jesus Christ. It was a personal encounter of the heart. Christ was revealed in him (not just to him but in him), and this happened not through any other human being but through a special revelation of Jesus Christ. Thus the experience itself is pure gift. We cannot control it, force it or make it happen. It is grace given when and where God wishes. We can only pray for it and hope for it. We can help to lead people into it. But it is not flesh and blood that reveals it. God can give it to anybody, anywhere, anytime. It is very much an inner experience. It is the gift of prayer in its deepest and purest form – an experience of the heart that is possible for everyone.

We find similar insights in this quotation from the *Spiritual Canticle* of St John of the Cross: 'You who so long to know the place where your beloved is, so as to seek him and become one with him, you yourself are the home in which he dwells ... Here is a reason to be happy; here is the cause for joy: the realisation that every blessing and all you hope for is so close to you as to be within you ... Be glad, find joy there, and be present to him who dwells within, since he is so close to you; desire him there, adore him there, and do not go off looking for him elsewhere. There is just one thing: even though he is within you, he is hidden. It is vital to know the place of his hiding, so that you can search for him with assuredness ... Since you know that in your heart, your beloved for whom you long, dwells hidden, your concern must be to be with him in hiding, and there in your heart you will embrace him.'

This is a wonderful description of what we mean by 'going the heart's way with Christ.'

*Please read the following slowly and prayerfully and pray that you will be able to recognise Christ present in your heart, soul and being. Also pray that you will not give up the search, even when he is hidden.*

### Galatians 1:11-21

For I want you to know, brothers and sisters, that the gospel that was proclaimed by me is not of human origin; for I did not receive it from a human source, nor was I taught it, but I received it through a revelation of Jesus Christ. When God, who had set me apart before I was born and called me through his grace, was pleased to reveal his Son to me [in me], so that I might proclaim him among the Gentiles, I did not confer with any human being, nor did I go up to Jerusalem to those who were already apostles before me, but I went away at once into Arabia, and afterwards I returned to Damascus. Then after three years I did go up to Jerusalem to visit Cephas and stayed with him fifteen days.

### Hymn
(Extract from *St Patrick's Breastplate*, trs Kuno Meyer)

Christ with me, Christ before me,
Christ behind me, Christ in me,
Christ beneath me, Christ above me
Christ on my right, Christ on my left.

Christ when I lie down, Christ when I sit down,
Christ when I arise, Christ to shield me,
Christ in the heart of everyone who thinks of me,
Christ in the mouth of everyone who speaks of me.

PART ONE: SECTION FOUR
'When Darkness Gathers'
*'May the light of Christ dispel
the darkness of our hearts and minds'*

## 4.1. A journey through darkness into light

On our journey into the mystery of God, we can encounter darkness and experience doubts. From time to time, our hearts can be heavy and our souls weary. We can expect this – so the spiritual writers tell us. Sometimes the light of faith is bright and clear but at other times the light can seem dim. At certain stages of the journey, we may feel 'it is good for us to be here' – wherever 'here' may be. While at other times the darkness closes in, the clouds come down and the fog surrounds us. This can fill us with fear and doubts. But we are encouraged to keep going; do not give up; persevere on the journey of faith, the journey into the mystery of God. It is then that we need to lift our eyes to the Lord, from where shall come our help. He is the light of the world; a light that shines in the darkness and the darkness cannot overcome it.

The experience of the three disciples on the mountain at the Transfiguration reveals many aspects of our journey into the mystery. They were 'on their own by themselves' and in a very privileged moment they saw Jesus being transfigured. It was a tremendous experience for them. They even wanted to remain there and hold on to the experience. But suddenly things changed. They discovered that darkness, doubt and even fear are never far away. They are part of the journey into the mystery. They were frightened and a cloud came, covering them with shadow. But this was the moment of deep revelation: From the cloud there came a voice: 'This is my Son, the beloved, listen to him.'

*Please read the following slowly and prayerfully. You may want to read it more than once. Then you can pick out some of the verses or phrases that have touched you deeply. Let them sink into your heart and being. Take time. Do not rush. Ask God to help you to live in the light all the days of your life.*

*Luke 9:28-36*

Jesus took with him Peter and John and James, and went up on the mountain to pray. And while he was praying, the appearance of his face changed, and his clothes became dazzling white. Suddenly they saw two men, Moses and Elijah, talking to him. They appeared in glory and were speaking of his departure, which he was about to accomplish at Jerusalem. Now Peter and his companions were weighed down with sleep; but since they had stayed awake, they saw his glory and the two men who stood with him. Just as they were leaving him, Peter said to Jesus, 'Master, it is good for us to be here; let us make three dwellings, one for you, one for Moses, and one for Elijah' – not knowing what he said. While he was saying this, a cloud came and overshadowed them; and they were terrified as they entered the cloud. Then from the cloud came a voice that said, 'This is my Son, my Chosen; listen to him!' When the voice had spoken, Jesus was found alone. And they kept silent and in those days told no one any of the things they had seen.

*Hymn*

O Christ the light of heaven
And of the world true light,
You come in all your radiance
To cleave the web of night.

May what is false within us
Before your truth give way,
That we may live untroubled,
With quiet hearts this day.
May steadfast faith sustain us,
And hope made firm in you;
The love that we have wasted,
O God of love, renew.

Blest Trinity we praise you
In whom our quest will cease;
Keep us with you forever
In happiness and peace. *(Stanbrook Abbey Hymnal)*

## 4.2. 'Oh night more loving than the dawn'

When we find ourselves journeying through the darkness, we try to remember that God is always close to us, loving us with an infinite love. People like John of the Cross and Teresa of Avila made the journey into the darkness and through the darkness back into the light. As they describe it, the darkness can be difficult and painful, but it is not a negative darkness. It is an inviting darkness. Because faith opens our minds and hearts to God, it can sometimes blind us. You can look directly at the stars, but if you look directly at the sun, it will blind you and you can see nothing for a while. The same happens when you switch on the light in a dark room. In faith, the darkness is there, not because God is distant, but because God is the infinite mystery, and there are times when we are blinded by the power, presence and light of our God.

St John of the Cross describes the darkness, the light and the love of the faith journey in his beautiful poems, especially in *The living flame of Love*, and *On a Dark Night* (given below). These poems are based on his own experience of his journey into the mystery of God. The focus is clearly on the living flame of love burning in his breast or heart, as he made the journey in stillness through the darkness into the light. For him the darkness was attractive and positive; it was a case of: 'oh night more loving than the dawn.' The poems convey a feeling of great warmth and intimacy in the relationship with God, as he experienced it on his own journey. The poems are full of images.

*Please read the scripture passage and the poem slowly and prayerfully and ask God to help you cope with the darkness and experience the light.*

*Colossians 1:9-14*
May you be made strong with all the strength that comes from his glorious power, and may you be prepared to endure everything with patience, while joyfully giving thanks to the Father, who has enabled you to share in the inheritance of the saints in

the light. He has rescued us from the power of darkness and transferred us into the kingdom of his beloved Son, in whom we have redemption, the forgiveness of sins.

*St John of the Cross: Stanzas Of The Soul (On a Dark Night)*[6]

> One dark night,
> fired with love's urgent longings
> – ah, the sheer grace! –
> I went out unseen,
> my house being now all stilled.
>
> In darkness, and secure,
> by the secret ladder, disguised,
> – ah, the sheer grace! –
> in darkness and concealment,
> my house being now all stilled.
>
> On that glad night,
> in secret, for no one saw me,
> nor did I look at anything,
> with no other light or guide
> than the one that burned in my heart.
>
> This guided me
> more surely than the light of noon
> to where he was awaiting me
> him I knew so well –
> there in a place where no one appeared.
>
> O guiding night!
> O night more lovely than the dawn!
> O night that has united the Lover
> with his beloved,
> transforming the beloved in her Lover.
> Upon my flowering breast

6. *The Collected Works of St. John of the Cross,* trs Kieran Kavanaugh, OCD and Otilio Rodriguez, ICS Publications, Washington,DC, 1973.

which I kept wholly for him alone,
there he lay sleeping,
and I caressing him
there in a breeze from the fanning cedars.

When the breeze blew from the turret,
as I parted his hair,
it wounded my neck with its gentle hand,
suspending all my senses.

I abandoned and forgot myself,
laying my face on my Beloved;
all things ceased; I went out from myself,
leaving my cares
forgotten among the lilies.
*(Poem of St John of the Cross)*

## 4.3. 'When darkness gathers, Christ's love is a fire'

On our pilgrim way through life, we are often left wondering what is happening and why is it happening when we encounter great darkness, suffering, loss and grief, in our own lives or the lives of those around us. It can even be the stare on the stranger's face that puts us in touch with the suffering and darkness in life. It is never far away. Kahlil Gibran wrote: 'Joy and sorrow go hand in hand in life, when one sits down at your table the other is asleep on your bed.' We can say the same about light and darkness as we journey into the mystery of God: light and darkness go hand in hand in life, when one sits down at your table, the other is asleep on your bed.

Christ identifies with us in our humanity, in our darkness and our suffering. He is with us at the heart of life. This is the wonder of the Incarnation. He became one of us and suffered and died for us, out of love.

Brother Roger of Taizé described how suffering can be redeemed by the flame of Christ's love: 'In every man and in every woman there is a wound, inflicted by failures, humiliations, bad conscience. Perhaps it was caused at a time when we needed infinite understanding, and acceptance, and nobody was there to give it ... transfigured by Christ, it is changed into a focus of energy... where communion, friendship and understanding burst forth.

For those who are marked by the suffering of the Cross of Christ, the day will come when they will be able to burn with the flame that is fed with their past life. They will know that in God nothing is lost ... when darkness gathers, his love is a fire!'

*Please read the following slowly and prayerfully and remember that 'Christ's gaze purifies our hearts; the light of his countenance illumines the eyes of our hearts and teaches us to see everything in the light of his truth and his compassion for all people' (CCC 2715)*

*Lk: 23: 39-43*

*(In this story, the words of Jesus to the criminal beside him reveal his compassion for all who experience darkness and distress and turn to him in their hearts. This is truly a moment of great significance for us. Far too often, doubts are sown in our minds and hearts about the amazing love and compassion that flows from the heart of Christ.)*

One of the criminals who were hanged there kept deriding him and saying, 'Are you not the Messiah? [or 'the Christ'] Save yourself and us!' But the other rebuked him, saying, 'Do you not fear God, since you are under the same sentence of condemnation? And we indeed have been condemned justly, for we are getting what we deserve for our deeds, but this man has done nothing wrong.' Then he said, 'Jesus, remember me when you come into your kingdom.' He replied, 'Truly I tell you, today you will be with me in Paradise.'

*Psalms 86*
*(Prayer in times of darkness)*

> Incline your ear, O Lord, and answer me,
> for I am poor and needy.
> Preserve my life, for I am devoted to you;
> save your servant who trusts in you.
> You are my God; be gracious to me, O Lord,
> for to you do I cry all day long.
>
> Gladden the soul of your servant,
> for to you, O Lord, I lift up my soul.
> For you, O Lord, are good and forgiving,
> abounding in steadfast love to all who call on you.
> Give ear, O Lord, to my prayer;
> listen to my cry of supplication.
> In the day of my trouble I call on you,
> for you will answer me.

There is none like you among the gods, O Lord,
nor are there any works like yours.
For you are great and do wondrous things;
you alone are God.
Teach me your way, O Lord,
that I may walk in your truth;
give me an undivided heart to revere your name.

I give thanks to you, O Lord my God, with my whole heart,
and I will glorify your name forever.
For great is your steadfast love toward me;
you have delivered my soul from the depths of Sheol.

You, O Lord, are a God merciful and gracious,
slow to anger and abounding in steadfast love
and faithfulness.
Turn to me and be gracious to me;
give your strength to your servant.

## 4.4. 'Lead kindly light, the night is dark'

We continue with the image of darkness and light and reflect how Christ delivers people from darkness. When I was in Kenya, I was amazed at the intensity of the darkness on certain nights. We were almost on the Equator where we were; a large yellow globe marked the spot a couple of kilometres down the road.

The sights and sounds of the tropical night are fascinating. I often lingered outside on the bright moonlit nights and found the experience so pleasant and calming. But there were nights in the rainy season when there is no moon and the clouds are down. Then the darkness is really intense. I sometimes stood and stared into the darkness. There is a kind of darkness behind the darkness. There is nothing I could see anywhere. On those dark nights there was no evidence of any life or world out there in the darkness or beyond the darkness.

It comes as no surprise that 'darkness' is a powerful symbol for people there. They certainly experience the darkness. The little light they have, when they have it, comes from a candle or a lantern – a storm lamp, as they call it. And of course there is another kind of darkness: suffering is very real. It is like a long dark shadow that covers their lives. In that area, as in so many parts of Africa, there is grinding poverty, disease and death on a large scale. Yet there can be such a sense of life and even joy and celebration in these small communities. The darkness and the light are never far apart. And people seem to manage to believe in the light. And there is little doubt that much of their sense of light and life comes from a deep spiritual faith in the mystery of God and his ways with them. It really means something to them when we talk about being delivered from the darkness of evil, sin and suffering. Christ's suffering, death and resurrection offer hope and comfort.

*Please read the following slowly and prayerfully and remember that 'Contemplative Prayer is a gaze of faith fixed on Jesus ... His gaze purifies our hearts; the light of his countenance illumines the eyes of our hearts and teaches us to see everything in the light of his truth and his compassion for all people' (CCC 2715).*

*Isaiah 9:2-6*
The people who walked in darkness have seen a great light; those who lived in a land of deep darkness – on them light has shined. You have multiplied the nation, you have increased its joy; they rejoice before you as with joy at the harvest, as people exult when dividing plunder. For the yoke of their burden, and the bar across their shoulders, the rod of their oppressor, you have broken as on the day of Midian. For all the boots of the tramping warriors and all the garments rolled in blood shall be burned as fuel for the fire. For a child has been born for us, a son given to us; authority rests upon his shoulders; and he is named Wonderful Counsellor, Mighty God, Everlasting Father, Prince of Peace.

*John 8:12*
Again Jesus spoke to them, saying, 'I am the light of the world. Whoever follows me will never walk in darkness but will have the light of life.'

*Hymn*
> Lead, kindly Light, amid the encircling gloom,
> lead thou me on;
> The night is dark, and I am far from home,
> lead thou me on.
> Keep thou my feet; I do not ask to see
> The distant scene; one step enough for me.
>
> I was not ever thus, nor prayed that
> thou shouldst lead me on;
> I loved to choose and see my path; but now
> lead thou me on.
> I loved the garish day, and, spite of fears,
> Pride ruled my will: remember not past years.

So long thy power hath blest me,
sure it still will lead me on
o'er moor and fen, o'er crag and torrent,
till the night is gone,
And with the morn those Angel faces smile,
Which I have loved long since, and lost awhile.
*(J. H. Newman 1801-1890)*

## 4.5. Jesus has a special care for the 'Lost'

We can also approach our theme of darkness and light from the experience of being 'lost'. Jesus saw his mission as revealing the merciful love of God to all; he had a special care for the 'lost' and the 'sinners'. He had great love for the poor, the meek and the downtrodden. The teaching of Jesus and his actions were a scandal to the religious authorities of his day. Jesus caused serious offence by seeking out sinners and eating with them. 'This fellow welcomes sinners and even eats with them!' (See Mark 2:16). His willingness to sit at table and eat with sinners was preaching to them in a very significant way. He gave hope to the outcasts who also knew it was against the law to eat with them. The scandal was that he associated with sinners and rejoiced in their company. He asked only that they accept his message, which offered them loving presence and forgiveness of God being revealed in Jesus himself. He calls them to repentance, which we need to understand in the manner of the prophets, as a response in love to God and as total devotion to God. On the whole, in contrast to John the Baptist, Jesus places the stress first on forgiveness; repentance follows from the encounter with Jesus. And Jesus turned forgiveness and repentance into a celebration. (Luke 15:7, 10, 22-24, 32). In these passages, there is no mention of penance or punishment.

Jesus visited the house of Levi and many others. He visits us too and calls us by name. He is at home with us and makes his home in us. He tells us: 'Make your home in me as I make mine in you' (Jn 15:4). Christ is always at home with us; there is no absence, no lack of love, no pulling away on his part. His light shines in the dark, lost corners of our hearts and lives.

St Paul reminds us that 'Nothing can separate us from the love of God that comes to us in Christ Jesus our Lord' (Rom 8:39). Ask God to help you to encounter Christ and experience his love and forgiveness, his light and peace in your heart.

*Please read the following slowly and prayerfully. You may want to read them a second time. Then you can pick out some of the verses or phrases that have touched you deeply. Let them sink into your heart and being. Take time. Do not rush.*

*Luke 5:27-39*
*(In this passage we find Jesus in the house of Levi, a tax collector. The scribes and Pharisees were never happy when Jesus made such visits. But Jesus makes it clear that he has come to call such people, so that he can reveal to them the mercy and compassion of the Father, who offers his forgiveness to all. He uses the visits and the meals to invite people to repent and be forgiven.)*

After this he went out and saw a tax collector named Levi, sitting at the tax booth; and he said to him, 'Follow me.' And he got up, left everything, and followed him. Then Levi gave a great banquet for him in his house; and there was a large crowd of tax collectors and others sitting at the table [Gk 'reclining'] with them. The Pharisees and their scribes were complaining to his disciples, saying, 'Why do you eat and drink with tax collectors and sinners?' Jesus answered, 'Those who are well have no need of a physician, but those who are sick; I have come to call not the righteous but sinners to repentance.'

*Hymn: 'A Touching Place'*[7]
*(This Hymn is focused on Christ's care for the lost and for all who suffer. We are called to follow his example)*

> Christ's is the world, in which we move,
> Christ's are the folk we are summoned to love,
> Christ's is the voice, which calls us to care,
> And Christ is the one who meets us here.
>
> To the lost Christ shows his face,
> To the unloved he gives his embrace,

---

7. 'A Touching Place' from *Love from Below* (Wild Goose Publications, 1988). Words John L. Bell and Graham Maule. Copyright 1998 WGRG, Iona Community, Glasgow G2 3DH, Scotland.

To those who cry in pain or disgrace,
Christ makes with his friends,
A touching place.

Feel for the people we most avoid,
Strange or bereaved or never employed;
Feel for the women and feel for the men,
who feel that their living is all in vain.

Feel for the parents who have lost their child;
Feel for the women whom men have defiled;
Feel for the baby, for whom there is no breast,
And feel for the weary who find no rest.

Feel for the lives by life confused,
riddled with doubt, in loving abused;
Feel for the lonely heart conscious of sin,
which longs to be pure, but fears to begin.

## 4.6. Jesus was deep into darkness and suffering

When we travel through the valley of darkness, our hope is grounded in Christ's love for us. Writing about 'Jesus Christ – The Incarnate Son of God,' Pope Benedict says that 'the divine loving activity of God takes on dramatic form when, in Jesus Christ, it is God himself who goes in search of the stray sheep, a suffering and lost humanity. When Jesus speaks in his parables of the shepherd who goes after the lost sheep, of the woman who looks for the lost coin, of the father who goes to meet and embrace his prodigal son, these are no mere words; they constitute an explanation of his very being and activity ... This is love in its most radical form.' (*God is Love*, 12)

Holy Week is an opportunity for us to feel and experience something of the pain and anguish that Christ endured for us, out of love. We feel for Christ as we journey with him through his last days and hours, as he endured the passion and crucifixion. We 'remember' the road he travelled. But 'remember' here has a special meaning. It means making present here and now what happened in the past. This allows us to enter into the experience itself in a deep way.

The more we can enter into all of this, the deeper will be our awareness of his love for us. The heart of Calvary is suffering and rejection but it is shot through with love and compassion.

Jesus suffered dreadful pain and great distress in Gethsemane. In the midst of his anguish we see his resignation and surrender to the Father's will: 'But let it be as you would have it, not as I ...' (Mk 14: 36). He was ready and willing to suffer and die for us.

There is also something else. Our contemplation of Christ's suffering in the past opens our hearts to suffering today. Jesus is present in each of us, as we re-live Calvary in our own experience. His identification with all who suffer is something we must contemplate deeply. This can make a real difference to our lives. It will touch our hearts and inspire us to help the countless people who are bowed down beneath the burden of poverty and suffering in today's world.

*Please read the following slowly and carefully and pray for the grace to be with Jesus as he shows us how great his love is, and how he willingly suffered for us to the point of death.*

*Lk 23:44-49*
*(Jesus was deep into suffering and darkness, as he endured his passion and crucifixion. And at the moment of his death, we are told that darkness covered the whole earth. Jesus entered into and shared our darkness and suffering. Through his passion, death and resurrection Jesus conquered sin, death and darkness and he is now our light and hope.)*
It was now about noon, and darkness came over the whole land until three in the afternoon, while the sun's light failed, and the curtain of the temple was torn in two. Then Jesus, crying with a loud voice, said, 'Father, into your hands I commend my spirit.' Having said this, he breathed his last. When the centurion saw what had taken place, he praised God and said, 'Certainly this man was innocent.' And when all the crowds who had gathered there for this spectacle saw what had taken place, they returned home, beating their breasts. But all his acquaintances, including the women who had followed him from Galilee, stood at a distance, watching these things.

*Conversation with Christ on the Cross*
St Ignatius suggests that we try to have a conversation with Christ on the Cross: 'Imagine Christ our Lord present before you upon the cross, and begin to speak with him, and listen to what he has to say to you. Then reflect on your own response to Christ's love' – A greater love than this no one has than to lay down one's life for one's friends – 'As I behold Christ in this plight, nailed to the cross, I shall ponder upon what presents itself to my mind and heart.'

This is one way to contemplate how much Christ loves us and how much he suffered for us. We can also journey with Christ by 'doing' the Stations of the Cross or by reading passages from the gospel accounts of Christ's passion.

*Prayer as we contemplate Christ on the Cross*

– Christ loves us so much that he suffered and died for us – may we experience his love in our hearts and lives.

– Christ prayed that we might be forgiven through his passion and death – may we experience his forgiveness and healing in areas where there is darkness and sin.

– Christ cried out in anguish: 'My God, My God, why have you forsaken me?' – may all who cry out in anguish find strength and comfort.

– Christ cried out: 'I thirst' – may we hear the cries of our brothers and sisters, when they cry to us for help.

– To the thief dying beside him, Jesus said: 'Truly I say to you, this day you will be with me in Paradise' – may these words be heard again by each of us when we are dying.

– Through John, his beloved disciple, Jesus gave us Mary to be our Mother – with her, we pray for ourselves and for all her children.

– Our loved ones have gone before us signed with the sign of the cross – may they rise with Christ in the light and peace of eternal glory.

– The crucified and Risen Christ is now the light of the world – may his light dispel the darkness of our hearts and minds.

## 4.7. God's forgiveness in Christ dispels the darkness

The forgiveness that comes through Christ dispels the darkness of our hearts and minds. In his preaching, John the Baptist called people to repentance because of the judgement that was approaching. With Jesus we have a different emphasis. The stress is more on forgiveness rather than repentance. Go back again to the very first words he preached, as recorded in St Mark: 'The time is fulfilled, and the kingdom of God is here; repent and believe in the good news' (Mark 1:15). While there is a call to repentance here, it is surely not the whole message. Jesus himself was not primarily a preacher of repentance; he proclaimed that the kingdom of God is here – that the saving power and loving presence of God is being made manifest in Christ himself and in our hearts, lives and world.

The one distinctive note that we can be certain marked the teaching of Jesus about the kingdom is that it would include 'sinners'. Jesus welcomed sinners without condition. The unconditional forgiveness of God is seen in Jesus. Jesus wants to reveal God as a merciful Father who welcomes the sinner home, as a good shepherd who searches for the lost sheep, as a woman who goes to great trouble searching for the lost coin.[8] These parables can be seen as focusing on repentance but also, and even more so, on the revelation of God's mercy and forgiveness.

The Psalmist lamented: 'How long will your hearts be closed? Will you love what is futile and seek what is false?' (Ps 4:2). Our attitudes and dispositions are clearly very important and especially our pride can prevent us from opening our hearts to the love, light and forgiveness of God. Jesus brings this home to his followers in one of the central stories recorded in Saint Luke's gospel: the story of the Pharisee and the tax collector. It illustrates how humble faith and trust in God enables us to be open to God's mercy and to be aware of our sinful state: 'Lord be merciful to me a sinner.' As the tax collector discovered, that little phrase is the key that opens our hearts to forgiveness, light and peace.

---

8. In this reflection, I am drawing on lectures given by Fr Wilfrid Harrington OP.

*Please read the following slowly and carefully and remember to ask God to help you to experience true forgiveness and repentance.*

*Luke 18:9-14*

He also told this parable to some who trusted in themselves that they were righteous and regarded others with contempt: 'Two men went up to the temple to pray, one a Pharisee and the other a tax collector. The Pharisee, standing by himself, was praying thus, "God, I thank you that I am not like other people: thieves, rogues, adulterers, or even like this tax collector. I fast twice a week; I give a tenth of all my income." But the tax collector, standing far off, would not even look up to heaven, but was beating his breast and saying, "God, be merciful to me, a sinner!" I tell you, this man went down to his home justified rather than the other; for all who exalt themselves will be humbled, but all who humble themselves will be exalted.'

*Psalms 40*
*(Prayer of thanks for Deliverance from the dark and desolate pit)*

> I waited patiently for the Lord;
> he inclined to me and heard my cry.
> He drew me up from the desolate pit,
> out of the miry bog,
> and set my feet upon a rock,
> making my steps secure.
> He put a new song in my mouth,
> a song of praise to our God.
> Many will see and fear,
> and put their trust in the Lord.
>
> Happy are those who make the Lord their trust,
> who do not turn to the proud,
> to those who go astray after false gods.
>
> I delight to do your will, O my God;
> your law is within my heart.
> I have told the glad news of deliverance

in the great congregation;
see, I have not restrained my lips, as you know, O Lord.
I have not hidden your saving help within my heart,
I have spoken of your faithfulness and your salvation;
I have not concealed your steadfast love
and your faithfulness
from the great congregation.

Do not, O Lord, withhold
your mercy from me;
let your steadfast love and your faithfulness
keep me safe forever.

Be pleased, O Lord, to deliver me;
O Lord, make haste to help me.

As for me, I am poor and needy,
but the Lord takes thought for me.
You are my help and my deliverer;
do not delay, O my God.

PART ONE: SECTION FIVE
# 'O Christ, that is what you have done'
*'O Christ, that is what you have done for us,*
*In a crumb of bread the whole mystery is.'*
(Patrick Kavanagh)

## 5.1. 'O Christ, that is what you have done for us'

In his Christmas meditation one year, the late Cardinal Hume told about a Londoner who was on his way home from work one evening before Christmas and felt drawn to Westminster Cathedral. He could not explain why, as he had long ago abandoned his faith. He may have drifted to church because he was feeling troubled. Having entered the building he came across the Christmas Crib. There were men, women and children all around, praying. He glanced at several of the faces of those at prayer. They seemed to be in possession of a precious secret. They looked at ease with themselves. He envied them. Then, turning away from the crib, his eyes settled on the large crucifix hanging from the dome of the Cathedral. He was quite taken aback at the sight of it – a man hanging on a cross, tortured, abandoned, dead.

The visitor sat and gazed at the crucifix. Slowly, it gave up its soul, its inner meaning. He began to see in the figure on the cross the faces of people suffering in the world: people slaughtered in Rwanda, people starving in Sudan – flies crawling all over their parched skin, eyes staring, no longer appealing for help, but waiting, just waiting for the end. He could see the grieving parents of loved ones killed in an accident, and the suffering of the mentally and physically sick. All human suffering seemed to be gathered up and made his own by the man on the cross.

Then he heard singing. It came from far away, from behind the main altar. It was quite beautiful. As he listened, his spirit seemed to be carried upwards into another sphere of reality; he soon realised that he was praying.

As the visitor left, an old man at the back of the cathedral wished him 'A Happy Christmas'. For the first time in his life, the visitor understood what it meant. He felt some peace and calm had entered his troubled heart; he felt much happier than he did when he arrived.

Later, the visitor would come to understand that the crib, the cross and the altar (the Eucharist) are all linked; the child in the manger is the same person as the man on the cross and the Risen Lord present in the Eucharist. He is our love and life, peace and hope. 'O Christ, that is what you have done for us.'

*Please read the following slowly and prayerfully and ask God to help you to come to know and experience what Christ has done for you.*

*Philippians 2:5-11*

Let the same mind be in you that was in Christ Jesus, who, though he was in the form of God, did not regard equality with God as something to be exploited, but emptied himself, taking the form of a slave, being born in human likeness. And being found in human form, he humbled himself and became obedient to the point of death – even death on a cross. Therefore God also highly exalted him and gave him the name that is above every name, so that at the name of Jesus every knee should bend, in heaven and on earth and under the earth, and every tongue should confess that Jesus Christ is Lord, to the glory of God the Father.

*Isaiah 12:1-6*
*(Great in your midst is the Holy One of Israel)*

You will say in that day:
I will give thanks to you, O Lord,
Surely God is my salvation;
I will trust, and will not be afraid,
for the Lord is my strength and my might;
he has become my salvation.

With joy you will draw water from the wells of salvation.
And you will say in that day:
Give thanks to the Lord,

call on his name;
make known his deeds among the nations;
proclaim that his name is exalted.

Sing praises to the Lord, for he has done gloriously;
let this be known in all the earth.
Shout aloud and sing for joy, O inhabitant of Zion,
for great in your midst is the Holy One of Israel.

## 5.2. The Risen Lord – Christ Our Light

The big fire was blazing not far from the church in Luanda, in western Kenya. It was a warm wet night. Fortunately, the rain had stopped a half an hour earlier. The darkness of the African night was intense. There were no lights to be seen anywhere in the surrounding countryside. This is the way it is every night. The homes all around us are in the dark. So, when there is no moon, you get a sense that the darkness is like a wall all around.

The fire and a few torches lit up the small area where we stood. So we began the celebration of the Easter Vigil – aware of the darkness and aware of the night. The Easter candle was blessed and lit from the fire. Our small candles were lit from the Easter candle and we processed into the church in the semi-darkness. The atmosphere was just right. The Easter candle and the small candles lit up the darkness. The prayers focused on darkness and light.

When the priest blessed the fire he prayed: 'Father, we share in the light of your glory, through your Son, the light of the world. Make this new fire holy … and bring us one day to the feast of eternal light, Amen.' As he lit the candle from the new fire, he prayed: 'May the light of Christ, rising in glory, dispel the darkness of our hearts and minds.' And when he lifted the Easter candle high in the air, he proclaimed: 'Christ our Light.'

As we moved through our celebration of the Easter Vigil in Luanda, the lights came on and there was so much life in the gathering of men, women and children; they sing, they dance, they clap, they pray, they sway to the tunes, they talk, and they laugh. There was a sense of joyful celebration and so much vitality that I have rarely experienced anywhere else. This is one of the mysteries of life in Africa. The people's joy in living is so tangible at times, despite all the suffering and hardship that is so much part of their lives. In people's lives, 'the many faces of the cross and suffering seem to go hand in hand with the many faces of joy and celebration.'

On that Holy Saturday night the people entered into the spirit of Easter with the kind of life and enthusiasm that left me filled with amazement. The Easter celebration seemed to have real meaning for them. People seemed to have a sense of 'what Christ had done for them.'

*Please Read the following slowly and prayerfully and take time to pray for deeper faith and trust in God as you journey into the mystery, since faith opens our hearts to the mystery of God revealed in the Risen Lord and the light of Easter. It is like a spark that lights up our lives in such a way that the Easter light comes shining through in creation and in human life, even in the most ordinary events and experiences*

### John 1:4-15

In him was life, and the life was the light of all people. The light shines in the darkness, and the darkness did not overcome it. There was a man sent from God, whose name was John. He came as a witness to testify to the light, so that all might believe through him. He himself was not the light, but he came to testify to the light. The true light, which enlightens everyone, was coming into the world. He was in the world, and the world came into being through him; yet the world did not know him. He came to what was his own, and his own people did not accept him. But to all who received him, who believed in his name, he gave power to become children of God, who were born, not of blood or of the will of the flesh or of the will of man, but of God. And the Word became flesh and lived among us, and we have seen his glory, the glory as of a father's only son, full of grace and truth.

### Hymn

Lord, God, your light which dims the stars
Awakes all things,
And all that springs to life in you,
Your glory sings.

Your peaceful presence, giving strength,
Is everywhere.

And fallen men may rise again
On the wings of prayer.

You are God whose mercy rests
On all you made;
You gave us Christ, whose love through death
our ransom paid.

We praise you, Father, with your Son
And Spirit blest,
In whom creation lives and moves
And finds its rest.
*(Stanbrook Abbey Hymnal)*

## 5.3. 'The presence, warmth and light of Christ'

This meditation is focused on the Eucharist as being really central and important to our lives. The whole mystery is present in this wonderful sacrament: 'O Christ, that is what you have done for us, In a crumb of bread the whole mystery is' (P. Kavanagh).

The celebration of the Eucharist is the centre, the source and summit of our Christian life, as the *Catechism of the Catholic Church* points out.

Jesus sits at table with sinners, Pharisees, ordinary people and his disciples. We too have to join him in order to strengthen our friendship with him and thus experience his healing power in our daily lives. The richness and depth of the Eucharist can only be grasped and lived by entering into an attitude of reflection and contemplation. This is the way we can come closer to Christ and deepen our love for him. This will help us to experience new life and light that will shine forth in our daily lives. It will enable us to bring the light and love of Christ to all we meet.

'The Eucharist should lead us to exclaim, as did the apostles after encountering him risen: "We have seen the Lord." The presence, warmth and light of Christ should remain with us and shine forth in our entire lives. Communion with Christ helps us to "see" the signs of the Divine presence in the world and to "manifest" it to all whom we encounter' (*The Year of the Eucharist*, 26).

And another quotation: 'The truth of our union with Jesus Christ in the Eucharist is tested by whether or not we love our fellow men and women; it is tested by how we treat others, especially our families: husbands and wives, children and parents, brothers and sisters. It is tested by whether or not we try to be reconciled to our enemies, or whether or not we forgive those who hurt and offend us. It is tested by whether we practise in life what our faith teaches us ... "you are my friends if you do what I command you". (Jn 15:14)' (Pope John Paul II in Ireland in 1979).

*Please read the following slowly and prayerfully and ask God to help you to come closer to Christ in the Eucharist. Remember that 'Contemplative Prayer is a gaze of faith fixed on Jesus ... His gaze purifies our hearts; the light of his countenance illumines the eyes of our hearts and teaches us to see everything in the light of his truth and his compassion for all people' (CCC 2715)*

*Philippians 3:7-18*
Yet whatever gains I had, these I have come to regard as loss because of Christ. More than that, I regard everything as loss because of the surpassing value of knowing Christ Jesus my Lord. For his sake I have suffered the loss of all things, and I regard them as rubbish, in order that I may gain Christ and be found in him, not having a righteousness of my own that comes from the law, but one that comes through faith in Christ, the righteousness from God based on faith. I want to know Christ and the power of his resurrection and the sharing of his sufferings by becoming like him in his death, if somehow I may attain the resurrection from the dead. Not that I have already obtained this or have already reached the goal; but I press on to make it my own, because Christ Jesus has made me his own. Beloved, I do not consider that I have made it my own; but this one thing I do: forgetting what lies behind and straining forward to what lies ahead, I press on toward the goal for the prize of the heavenly call of God in Christ Jesus. Let those of us then who are mature be of the same mind; and if you think differently about anything, this too God will reveal to you. Only let us hold fast to what we have attained. Brothers and sisters, join in imitating me, and observe those who live according to the example you have in us.

*Paul's Prayer in Ephesians 1:3-13*
*(Our Spiritual Blessings in Christ)*
Blessed be the God and Father of our Lord Jesus Christ, who has blessed us in Christ with every spiritual blessing in the heavenly places, just as he chose us in Christ before the foundation of the world to be holy and blameless before him in love.

He destined us for adoption, as his children through Jesus Christ, according to the good pleasure of his will, to the praise of his glorious grace that he freely bestowed on us in the Beloved.

In him we have redemption through his blood, the forgiveness of our trespasses, according to the riches of his grace that he lavished on us. With all wisdom and insight he has made known to us the mystery of his will, according to his good pleasure that he set forth in Christ, as a plan for the fullness of time, to gather up all things in him, things in heaven and things on earth.

In Christ we have also obtained an inheritance, having been destined according to the purpose of him who accomplishes all things according to his counsel and will, so that we, who were the first to set our hope on Christ, might live for the praise of his glory.

## 5.4. 'We want Jesus to walk where we walk'

In the Holy Eucharist, we are offered the opportunity to encounter the Crucified and Risen Lord in a most personal way, when we receive him and welcome him into our hearts. The wonder of the Eucharist is at the heart of our experience of God's infinite love for us. Our encounter with Christ in the Eucharist bears fruit in our lives. It leads to change and transformation at a personal level, but also at the level of the society in which we live. Our desire for change and transformation is summed up in the words of the hymn: 'Our selfish hearts make new, our failing faith renew, our lives belong to you, our Lord and King.'

As the bread and wine are changed into the Body and Blood of Christ, so too will we be changed, by being drawn closer to Christ and into Christ. We cannot live as Christians without Christ. We are all part of the Body of Christ. And here we have our social responsibilities that flow from our participation in the Eucharist. St John Chrysostom, one of the early doctors of the church, wrote: 'Do you wish to honour the body of Christ? Do not ignore him when he is naked. Do not pay him homage in the temple clad in silk, only then to neglect him outside where his cold and ill-clad.' He who said 'This is my body' is the same who said 'You saw me hungry and you gave me food' and 'Whatsoever you did to the least of my brothers and sisters, you did also to me.'

There must always be this link between the Eucharist we celebrate and the life we live. The bread from heaven has to be submerged in our everyday life – as Pope Benedict puts it: 'We want Jesus to walk where we walk, to live where we live; our world, our lives, must become his temple.'

*Please read the following slowly and prayerfully and remember that 'Contemplative Prayer is a gaze of faith fixed on Jesus … His gaze purifies our hearts; the light of his countenance illumines the eyes of our hearts and teaches us to see everything in the light of his truth and his compassion for all people' (CCC 2715) Ask Jesus to walk where you walk and to live where you live.*

*Instead of a Scripture passage we can take the following:*

On the Feast of Corpus Christi, 2005, Pope Benedict led the annual procession through the streets of Rome. His homily on that day dwelt on the meaning of the Eucharist. It is, he said, the secret of charity in the church, a treasure and a precious heritage not only for the baptised but given for the life of the world.

The Corpus Christi Procession that he led through Rome was full of meaning, he said, because it signified the submerging of the bread descended from heaven into our everyday life: We want Jesus to walk where we walk, to live where we live; our world, our lives, must become his temple.

The Eucharist, he added, is the very life of a Christian community, the source of love that triumphs over death. At the procession, the Pope called the Eucharist a 'synthesis of creation' and ended his homily with the following prayer:

'Show anew the just path to the church and her shepherds!
Look at suffering humanity, which wanders uncertain amid so many questions; look at the physical and psychic hunger that torments it! Give them bread for the body and soul! Give them work! Give them light! Give them yourself! Purify and sanctify us all!'

In closing, the Holy Father prayed: 'Make us understand that only through participation in your passion, through the "eyes" of the Cross, of denial, of the purification that you impose on us, our lives can mature and reach their authentic fulfilment.'

*Preface of Corpus Christi*
*(The Eucharist helps us 'to walk in the light of faith, in one communion of love')*

Father, all-powerful and ever-living God,
we do well always and everywhere to give you thanks
through Jesus Christ our Lord.
At the last supper,
as he sat at table with his apostles,
he offered himself to you as the spotless lamb,
the acceptable gift that gives you perfect praise.

Christ has given us this memorial of his passion
to bring us its saving power until the end of time.
In this great sacrament you feed your people
and strengthen them in holiness,
so that the family of mankind
may come to walk in the light of one faith,
in one communion of love.
We come then to this wonderful sacrament
to be fed at your table
and grow into the likeness of the risen Christ.
Earth unites with heaven
to sing the new song of creation
as we adore and praise you for ever.

## 5.5. The wind in our sails

The image of a sailing ship can help us to understand the effect of the presence and activity of the Spirit of Christ (the Holy Spirit) in our lives – what Christ does for us.

Try to imagine a sailing ship helplessly drifting with the current at the mouth of the harbour. It is waiting for a breeze. Then it comes, a powerful wind fills the limp and lifeless sails. The tall ship begins to move with definite intent. Soon it is headed out into the open sea, leaving the safety of the harbour well behind. It powers its way out into the deep ocean. And so it is with us. The Holy Spirit fills our sails and powers us forward on our journey into the depths of the mystery of God.

The Holy Spirit has one desire or purpose, namely, to draw us closer to Christ, to unite us with him and to make us one with him – to create in us the image of Christ. Through the presence of the Holy Spirit we become children of God and brothers and sisters of Jesus Christ.

The Spirit is at the heart of a 'movement', which takes place within the human spirit. We all reflect as in a mirror the splendour of the Lord; thus we are transfigured into his likeness, such is the influence of the Lord who is Spirit (2 Cor 3:18). We become one with Christ, we are moulded into his image, under the influence of and through the energy that is the Spirit. As a result, 'everyone who is united to Christ is one Spirit with him' (1 Cor 6:17). And 'I live now, no longer I, but Christ lives in me' (Gal 2:20).

We want to feel the touch of the Spirit deep within our being, since: 'the love of God has been poured into our hearts, through the Holy Spirit given to us'. (Rom 5:5) This is what we celebrate at Pentecost: the outpouring of God's spirit into our hearts and into the whole of creation.

*Please read the following scripture passage and hymn slowly and prayerfully and pray for deeper faith in Christ and his Holy Spirit, since faith alone is the key that opens our hearts to the beauty of God.*

*Romans 8:14-17*

For all who are led by the Spirit of God are children of God. For you did not receive a spirit of slavery to fall back into fear, but you have received a spirit of adoption. When we cry, 'Abba! Father!' it is that very Spirit bearing witness with our spirit that we are children of God, and if children, then heirs, heirs of God and joint heirs with Christ – if, in fact, we suffer with him so that we may also be glorified with him.

*Hymn*

A mighty wind invades the world,
So strong and free on beating wing:
It is the Spirit of the Lord,
From whom all truth and freedom spring.

The Spirit is a fountain clear,
For ever leaping to the sky,
Whose waters give unending life,
Whose timeless source is never dry.

The Spirit comes in tongues of flame,
With love and wisdom burning bright,
The wind, the fountain and the fire
Combine in this great feast of light.

O tranquil Spirit, bring us peace,
With God the Father and the Son.
We praise you, blessed Trinity,
Unchanging, and for ever One.
*(Stanbrook Abbey Hymnal)*

## 5.6. The fire in the ashes

We can reflect on another image for what Christ does for us through the presence of his Spirit. When I was growing up we had an 'open fire' at home. This was the way it was for nearly every home in our part of the country. There were very few ranges or stoves of any kind. There was just the open hearth and the big chimney that carried the smoke – and some of the heat as well. The fuel burned was turf, which was harvested from the peat bog nearby. Sometimes a log was placed at the back of the fire; it burned more slowly than turf.

As the night wore on the fire went down and the fire eventually amounted to hot coals and a lot of ashes. I remember well a little ritual that was repeated each night at bedtime; it was a task reserved for an adult. My mother or father would kindle the fire: this was the process of burying the remains of the fire in ashes; the hot coals were carefully preserved in a bed of ashes and covered over with ashes. You could no longer see the fire or feel the heat; the glowing coals remained hidden overnight; they were referred to as 'grieshog'.

The next morning the ashes was cleared away, the hot coals were rescued and a new fire was quickly started; soon the warmth, light and energy coming from the fire was there once again, for all in the house to enjoy. As a matter of fact, I was surprised to find a similar custom in the part of Kenya where I have spent the last ten years. They still preserve the fire in this way.

This custom can serve as an image for the presence of the Holy Spirit in our hearts. The hidden fire, the night, the ashes concealing the fire, the darkness all around, are all useful images when we try to imagine the activity of the Holy Spirit.

Like the 'grieshog' (the hidden fire), the spark of the Divine is alive in each person. The Holy Spirit is present and active in our human hearts and has one desire: to draw us closer to Christ, to unite us with him and to make us one with him.

In the words of *Redemtoris Missio*, 'The love of God, the Spirit of God, is present in peoples' hearts, in their history, in their culture, and in their religion. The Holy Spirit, with his gifts, is there waiting for the person to awaken to the reality; the task is to discover those gifts, receive them with dialogue and foster them.'[9]

This is a good description of what we mean by 'going the heart's way'.

*Please read the following slowly and prayerfully and pray 'Come Holy Spirit, fill my heart.'*

*Galatians 5:16-26*
Live by the Spirit, I say, and do not gratify the desires of the flesh. For what the flesh desires is opposed to the Spirit, and what the Spirit desires is opposed to the flesh; for these are opposed to each other, to prevent you from doing what you want. But if you are led by the Spirit, you are not subject to the law. Now the works of the flesh are obvious: fornication, impurity, licentiousness, idolatry, sorcery, enmities, strife, jealousy, anger, quarrels, dissensions, factions, envy, drunkenness, carousing, and things like these. I am warning you, as I warned you before: those who do such things will not inherit the kingdom of God.

By contrast, the fruit of the Spirit is love, joy, peace, patience, kindness, generosity, faithfulness, gentleness, and self-control. There is no law against such things. And those who belong to Christ Jesus have crucified the flesh with its passions and desires. If we live by the Spirit, let us also be guided by the Spirit. Let us not become conceited, competing against one another, envying one another.

*Hymn*
> Come, Holy Ghost, creator,
> come from thy bright heavenly throne,
> come, take possession of our souls,
> and make them all thine own.
>
> Thou who art called the Paraclete,
> best gift of God above,

---

9. *Redemptoris Missio*, Numbers 28 and 29.

the living spring, the living fire,
sweet unction and true love.

Thou who art sevenfold in thy grace,
finger of God's right hand;
his promise, teaching little ones
to speak and understand.

O guide our minds with thy blest light,
with love our hearts inflame;
and with thy strength, which ne'er decays,
confirm our mortal flame.

Far from us drive our deadly foe;
true peace unto us bring;
and through all perils lead us safe
beneath thy sacred wing.

Through thee may we the Father know,
through thee the eternal Son,
and thee the Spirit of them both,
thrice-blessed Three in One.

All glory to the Father be,
with his co-equal Son;
the same to thee, great Paraclete,
while endless ages run.
*(Ascribed to Rabanus Maurus)*

## 5.7. 'Within the shelter of the Trinity'

In the loving God revealed in Christ, we come face to face with a Trinity of Persons. We believe that God has been revealed: as Father, who is the Creator and sustainer of life; as Son, who is the redeemer of all humanity; and as Holy Spirit who is the sanctifier and our bond of love. This is the mystery of the Holy Trinity that Christ reveals to us, as he draws us into its life and love. This is what Christ does for us.

Some years ago, a story was doing the rounds. The bishop came for confirmation and he was asking questions of the children in the church before the celebration. He asked one boy: 'What is the Trinity?' The boy gave a quick answer but it was very indistinct. The bishop then said that he did not understand and the boy replied: 'You are not supposed to understand, my Lord, because it is a mystery.' I am sure that the bishop was not too impressed, even though the boy was not far wrong. The Trinity is ultimate mystery and finally escapes an adequate understanding or expression. But Christ takes us into the depths of that mystery; that is what he has done for us.

The Trinity is very much part of our daily lives. Many times a day we sign ourselves with the Sign of the Cross and bless ourselves in the name of the Father and of the Son and of the Holy Spirit. In 'blessing ourselves' we arise each day with the strength of heaven and we place the circle of our lives within the shelter of the Trinity (An old Irish prayer). As we touch the forehead, we do so in the name of the Father, the source of life and vision. As we touch the chest (heart) we do so in the name of the Son, the source of mercy and compassion. As we touch the left and right shoulders, we do so in the name of the Holy Spirit, the source of love and holiness.

St Ignatius of Loyola had great devotion to the Holy Trinity and on one occasion, while he was praying, he got an insight into the Trinity and 'saw' the three Divine Persons as three keys of a keyboard instrument. He also 'heard' the harmony of their music. He was filled with joy and great delight. His devotion to the most Holy Trinity permeated his life and his spiritual writings.

*Please read the following slowly and prayerfully and ask God to help you to enter more deeply into the mystery of the Trinity and to 'place the circle of your life within the shelter of the Trinity.'*

*Matthew 28:16-20*
Now the eleven disciples went to Galilee, to the mountain to which Jesus had directed them. When they saw him, they worshiped him; but some doubted. And Jesus came and said to them, 'All authority in heaven and on earth has been given to me. Go therefore and make disciples of all nations, baptising them in the name of the Father and of the Son and of the Holy Spirit, and teaching them to obey everything that I have commanded you. And remember, I am with you always, to the end of the age.'

*Hymn*[10]
*(We have used this hymn in Reflection 2. I want to use it here again because of the way it describes the Trinity as a community of love. The hymn is based on the writings of St Ignatius.)*

The Father loves the Son with all the love he is;
The Son responds with loving as total as his;
The Spirit is the living love of Father and Son,
Receiving and giving their three love as one.

How can a love so total say anything to me?
How can love be so selfless – so totally free?
How can love be a spirit our eyes cannot see?
How can love speak love's meaning to you and to me?

The love of the Father took flesh in the Son;
The love of the Son still lives on his friends;
The love of the Spirit is born in each heart,
Awaiting, awakening when rocks break apart.

---

10. From *Inigo – Story and Songs*, by William Hewitt SJ (Inigo Enterprises, 'Inigo's Place' Links View, Traps Lane, New Malden, Surrey KT3 4RY. www.inigonet.org)

Lord Jesus Christ, my King, my Sun,
You are the source whence love's rays come;
You shine through all things, your loving flows.
Through bread and wine, your presence grows.

I sense your light in every ray;
I see you shape each break of day;
In Bread and Wine though our eyes can't see,
I sense your love enliven me.

I see your rays one with the sun;
I see them reach to everyone;
In Bread and Wine Lord remembered be;
transform our lives, Lord make us free.

The river runs deep along my road;
it hums its song, makes light my load;
It leads me on beyond my fears;
it opens locks, releases tears.

Your river runs deep within my heart
releases springs in deepest parts.
It leads me on to spaces new,
it opens gates, lets flow what's true.

Our river runs deep, my heart is full,
your song flows through each depth I feel;
I know you are here wherever I go:
Lord, may our river ever flow.

PART ONE: SECTION SIX
'The Unbreakable Bond'
*'Act justly, love tenderly,*
*walk humbly with your God'* (Micah 6:8)

## 6.1. 'The Unbreakable Bond'

There is an unbreakable bond between all areas of Christian life: love of God, love of self, love of others and respect for creation. A loving heart is the home of this bond. It is the anchor for the love that is lived out in each area of relationship – as we 'go the heart's way.'

The journey of faith, the Christian life, is always a response to Christ's love in our hearts and lives. The personal encounter of the heart with Christ is being lived out in daily living.

This is the context in which we understand the call of Christ, to believe the good news that the kingdom (love) of God is here, and to repent and be converted (Mk 1:14-15). We find the same thing expressed in another way, in the invitation of Jesus to love the Lord your God with all your heart, with all your soul, with all your strength and with your entire mind and to love your neighbour as yourself (Lk 10:27). We are called to grow towards maturity in a loving relationship with God, self and others. Love of God, self and others involves respect for others. It leads us into the area of justice, human rights and respect for creation and the environment. This latter area is not explicitly covered in the text from Luke but we can find plenty of references all through the Bible. Probably one of the best is the verse from the prophet Micah that tells us we are called to act justly, to love tenderly and to walk humbly with your God (Micah 6:8).

All relationships are important in our Christian life. They are part of an integrated or balanced spirituality. While allowing for personal interest, each area has to be attended to and problems arise if we ignore one or more of them. Writing about the call to love God and neighbour, Pope Benedict notes that: 'The unbreakable bond between love of God and love of neighbour is emphasised in the First Letter of John. One is so closely connected to the other that to say we love God becomes a lie if we are closed to our neighbour or hate him altogether. St John's words should be interpreted to mean that love of neighbour is a path that leads to the encounter with God, and that closing our eyes to our neighbour also blinds us to God.'[11]

When we talk about Christian love in the context of relationships, we need to remember what St Augustine said: 'The love with which we love one another is the same love with which God loves us.' Ask God to help you to love him with all your heart, and to love your neighbour as yourself.'

*Please read the following slowly and prayerfully and remember that 'the fruit of silence is prayer. The fruit of prayer is faith. The fruit of faith is love. The fruit of love is service. The fruit of service is peace (Mother Teresa).*

*Luke 10:29-37*
But wanting to justify himself, he asked Jesus, 'And who is my neighbour?' Jesus replied, 'A man was going down from Jerusalem to Jericho, and fell into the hands of robbers, who stripped him, beat him, and went away, leaving him half dead. Now by chance a priest was going down that road; and when he saw him, he passed by on the other side. So likewise, a Levite, when he came to the place and saw him, passed by on the other side. But a Samaritan while travelling came near him; and when he saw him, he was moved with pity. He went to him and bandaged his wounds, having poured oil and wine on them. Then he put him on his own animal, brought him to an inn, and took care of him. The next day he took out two denarii, {The denarius was the usual day's wage for a labourer} gave them to the innkeeper, and said, "Take care of him; and when I come back, I will repay you whatever more you spend." Which of these three, do you think, was a neighbour to the man who fell into the hands of the robbers?' He said, 'The one who showed him mercy.' Jesus said to him, 'Go and do likewise.'

11. Pope Benedict's encyclical *God is Love*, Number 16.

*Hymn*

> Come, Holy Spirit, live in us
> With God the Father and the Son,
> And grant us your abundant grace
> To sanctify and make us one.
>
> May mind and tongue made strong in love,
> Your praise throughout the world proclaim,
> And may that love within our hearts
> Set fire to others with its flame.
>
> Most Blessed Trinity of love,
> For whom the heart of man was made,
> To you be praise in timeless song,
> And everlasting homage paid.

## 6.2. Love blossoms in a compassionate heart

Love of God and others (with the unbreakable bond between them) blossoms in a compassionate heart. Many of us have seen and experienced love and compassion in our lives. We can be very aware of this when we journey through suffering, grief and loss. When we have had the experience of losing a loved one, we are well aware of the sense of pain and loss that it brings. Even when it is a parent of advanced age there is still a deep sense of grief and mourning. But, for many of us, there is also another side to the experience. It can be a time when we come to know the love of family and friends in a new way. I am well aware that the opposite can also happen. Family feuds are frequent enough around the funeral of a loved one. Thankfully, more often there is a great outpouring of friendship and support from family members, friends and neighbours. This is especially true when it is a sudden death of a younger person through illness or a tragic accident or even worse still, through suicide. Any of these, espe-cially the case of suicide, leaves family members devastated and bewildered. It is hard to imagine what people in such a situation go through. You can even wonder how people cope with such a tragedy. As they struggle with the tragic loss, the grief and all the pain and anguish, they seem to get strength from some-where. And in some situations they are greatly helped by the tremendous outpouring of love and compassion from family, friends and neighbours. Such tragedies bring out the best in peo-ple. You can see love and compassion in action, at the deepest level. Love of others takes on a new dimension.

Perhaps 'compassion' is the best word to describe the love that is expressed and experienced at such times. The word 'love' is not adequate to describe what is happening; it is used, even over-used and abused these days. So 'compassion' may be the better word. It is more appropriate for love at its deepest level. It really means 'to suffer with' or to 'enter into the suffering of an-other person and journey with them.' This is the love that people come to know and experience in the tragic situations of life – and if you are lucky enough in normal life also. It is the love that

Pope Benedict refers to when he writes about love in his encyclical, *God is Love*. It is the love that we are capable of because God's love has been poured into our hearts; it is a love that is willing to give, to sacrifice and to suffer with another person. This is what we mean by love as 'compassion.' Pope Benedict assures us that this love can blossom within us, in a compassionate human heart.[12]

*Please read the following slowly and prayerfully and ask God to fill your heart with compassion.*

*Colossians 3:12-17*
As God's chosen ones, holy and beloved, clothe yourselves with compassion, kindness, humility, meekness, and patience. Bear with one another and, if anyone has a complaint against another, forgive each other; just as the Christ has forgiven you, so you also must forgive. Above all, clothe yourselves with love, which binds everything together in perfect harmony. And let the peace of Christ rule in your hearts, to which indeed you were called in the one body. And be thankful. Let the word of Christ dwell in you richly; teach and admonish one another in all wisdom; and with gratitude in your hearts sing psalms, hymns, and spiritual songs to God. And whatever you do, in word or deed, do everything in the name of the Lord Jesus, giving thanks to God the Father through him.

*Psalm 103:13-22*
*(God's compassionate love)*

> As a father has compassion for his children,
>  so the Lord has compassion for those who fear him.
> For he knows how we were made;
>  he remembers that we are dust.
>
> As for mortals, their days are like grass;
>  they flourish like a flower of the field;

---

12. Pope Benedict's encyclical *God is Love*, Number 17.

for the wind passes over it, and it is gone,
and its place knows it no more.

But the steadfast love of the Lord is
from everlasting to everlasting on those who fear him,
and his righteousness to children's children,
to those who keep his covenant
and remember to do his commandments.

The Lord has established his throne in the heavens,
and his kingdom rules over all.
Bless the Lord, O you his angels,
you mighty ones who do his bidding,
obedient to his spoken word.

Bless the Lord, all his hosts,
his ministers that do his will.
Bless the Lord, all his works,
in all places of his dominion.
Bless the Lord, O my soul.

## 6.3 A forgiving heart

A compassionate heart is a forgiving heart. There is an unbreakable bond here. Our ability to forgive is rooted in a compassionate heart that has been touched and awakened by God's gracious love and forgiveness.

The story of the Prodigal Son can help us here. The first part of the story portrays God's gracious forgiveness. The sinner was warmly welcomed and reinstated without condition. The second part centres on the other son, the righteous one; he was scandalised and hurt. It is not fair! This was his mistake: he had not understood that God is not fair! God is wholly merciful and boundless in his forgiveness. This even outweighs our sense of fairness and justice. The Father who had embraced the sinner is gentle, too, with the aggrieved righteous one. 'Son, you are always with me, and all that is mine is yours.' He is in no sense worse off because God is merciful. What is in question is recognition of a merciful God. The elder son had washed his hands of his brother. The unwelcome home-comer was this son of yours! He is, by his father, delicately but unmistakably put right: the home-comer is this brother of yours. And he was invited to enter into the celebration: 'We had to celebrate and rejoice.'

The ending of the story leaves us with a situation that is not resolved. Its purpose is to involve the reader or hearer. We are made to wonder how we might act in the place of the elder brother. Will I stay outside, sulking? Will I welcome my sister or brother and share the joy of our Father? In effect, I must write the ending of this story. My ending will depend on my understanding of God – my image of God. Is God a merciful Father for me? It will also depend on whether I identify with the merciful Father or the prodigal son or the elder brother or am I somewhere in between?[13]

Whether you see yourself as the prodigal son or the elder brother, take time to pray for a profound awareness of God's love and forgiveness; this will lead to an abiding sorrow for sin,

13. In this reflection, I am drawing on lectures given by Fr Wilfrid Harrington OP.

and a turning away from sin. These are the two dimensions of repentance, conversion, which can best be described as a change of heart that leads to deep personal transformation. Pray for an experience of reconciliation with God, with others and even with your own self. There is an unbreakable bond here that comes about through a compassionate and forgiving heart, centred on Christ. Remember: 'Those who refuse to forgive, break the bridge over which they themselves must cross' *(African Proverb)*.

*Please read the following scripture passage and psalm slowly and prayerfully. You may want to read them more than once. Then you can pick out some of the verses or phrases that have touched you deeply. Let them sink into your heart and being. Take time.*

*Luke 15:25-32*
Now his elder son was in the field; and when he came and approached the house, he heard music and dancing. He called one of the slaves and asked what was going on. He replied, 'Your brother has come, and your father has killed the fatted calf, because he has got him back safe and sound.' Then he became angry and refused to go in. His father came out and began to plead with him. But he answered his father, 'Listen! For all these years I have been working like a slave for you, and I have never disobeyed your command; yet you have never given me even a young goat so that I might celebrate with my friends. But when this son of yours came back, who has devoured your property with prostitutes, you killed the fatted calf for him!' Then the father [Gk 'he'] said to him, 'Son, you are always with me, and all that is mine is yours. But we had to celebrate and rejoice, because this brother of yours was dead and has come to life; he was lost and has been found.'

*Psalm 51*
*(Prayer for a pure, contrite and forgiving heart)*

Have mercy on me, O God, according to your steadfast love;
according to your abundant mercy,
blot out my transgressions.
Wash me thoroughly from my transgressions,
And cleanse me from my sin.

For I know my transgressions,
and my sin is ever before me.
Against you, you alone, have I sinned.

You desire truth in the inward being;
therefore teach me wisdom in my secret heart.

Create in me a pure heart, O God,
and put a new and right spirit within me.
Do not cast me away from your presence,
And do not take your Holy Spirit from me.

Restore to me the joy of your salvation,
And sustain in me a willing spirit.

The sacrifice acceptable to God is a contrite spirit;
a humble and contrite heart, O God, you will not despise.

O Lord, open my lips and I will declare your praise.

## 6.4. 'To be called is to be sent'

As disciples of Christ, we are called to reach out to all in love and service, mission and witness. There is an unbreakable bond between love, service, mission and witness. These are all central to 'going the heart's way'.

'To be called is to be sent' is a popular Swahili saying, which is used in different settings in East Africa. Among the Logir people in Sudan, there is a custom of the leaders or elders of the community calling for a person in the middle of the night, or very early in the morning. The person is then sent on a specific mission, which is usually connected with rituals and religious ceremonies. Hence, to be called is to be sent. The expression is also used during the Easter Vigil Service in East Africa; the newly-baptised are instructed with the saying 'To be called is to be sent.' The meaning of this is that Christ and the Christian community first call them, and then they are sent out to witness, in service and mission.

'To be called is to be sent' sums up rather well the unbreakable bond between our call to discipleship and our call to witness to Christ in today's world. Christ calls us to a personal relationship with himself that moves on to discipleship, witness, mission and ministry.

In the passage from Mark given below, we read: 'Jesus called to himself those whom he wanted, and they came to him.' The phrase *called to himself* is common enough in Mark and expresses the closeness of the relationship that Jesus has with his disciples. Apparently the word 'want' can also be translated as 'to have someone at heart'. Jesus thus calls to himself, to the way of discipleship, those whom he wants and those whom he has at heart. And they came to him – literally, they went close to him and were to be his companions and to be sent out. These little phrases have great significance. Teresa Clements notes: 'It is the actual being with Jesus himself, in an intimate relationship with him, that leads the disciples to witness and proclaim the good news to others and to have power over evil.'

Thus closeness to Christ is central; the rest flows from it. It is interesting to note that the early Celtic missionaries were 'pilgrims for Christ' – they left home and country in order to be closer to Christ: 'It was the love of Christ and their seeking of Christ that was the impulse behind their movement.' Once they were in their new countries, they responded to the spiritual needs of those around them and conversions to Christ followed.[14] So we are called to be close to Christ and we are sent out by Christ and Christ is always there ahead of us, waiting to welcome us, wherever *there* may be.

*Please read the following slowly and carefully and pray for the grace to be close to Christ in prayer and to be together with him in loving service, in mission and ministry.*

*Mark 3:13-17*
He went up the mountain and called to himself those whom he wanted, and they came to him. He appointed twelve, whom he also named apostles, to be with him, and to be sent out to proclaim the message, and to have authority to cast out demons. So he appointed the twelve apostles …

*Redemptoris Missio:*
'It is precisely because he or she is 'sent' that the missionary experiences the consoling presence of Christ, who is with him or her at every moment of life … and who awaits the arrival of the missionary in the heart of every person. The Spirit of Christ is present and active in every time and place' (28, 18).

14. See Teresa Clements, *Missionary Spirituality*, Vol 31, *Living Flame*, Carmelite, Dublin, 1987, pp 14, 16, 27.

*Hymn: 'A Touching Place'*[15]
*(This hymn (which we have used in an earlier reflection) sums up the importance of friendship with Christ that enables us to reach out to others in love and service, mission and ministry.)*

Christ's is the world in which we move,
Christ's are the folk we are summoned to love,
Christ's is the voice which calls us to care,
and Christ is the one who meets us here.

To the lost Christ shows his face,
To the unloved he gives his embrace,
To those who cry in pain or disgrace,
Christ makes with his friends,
A touching place.

Feel for the people we most avoid,
Strange or bereaved or never employed;
Feel for the women and feel for the men,
who feel that their living is all in vain.

Feel for the parents who have lost their child;
Feel for the women whom men have defiled;
Feel for the baby for whom there is no breast,
And feel for the weary who find no rest.

Feel for the lives by life confused,
riddled with doubt, in loving abused;
Feel for the lonely heart conscious of sin,
which longs to be pure, but fears to begin.

15. 'A Touching Place' from *Love from Below* (Wild Goose Publications, 1988). Words John L. Bell and Graham Maule. Copyright 1998 WGRG, Iona Community, Glasgow G2 3DH, Scotland.

## 6.5. 'Act justly, love tenderly and walk humbly with God'

There is an unbreakable bond between commitment to Christ and concern for justice and peace; this includes respect for creation and concern about the environment, global warming, and climate change.

Some years ago I wrote an article in *Saint Joseph's Advocate*, our Mill Hill magazine, in which I quoted the text from the prophet Micah (6:8): 'This is what the Lord God asks of you: to act justly, to love tenderly and to walk humbly with your God.' Some time later I got a letter from an elderly man, who thanked me for drawing his attention to such a wonderful verse of scripture. He went on to say that he found it extremely helpful and that it is the best advice that any parent or teacher could offer to the young generation.

Micah 6:8 gives us deep insights into 'going the heart's way'. It is a summary of the message of three of the great prophets. We find Amos's demand for justice, Hosea's appeal for steadfast love that binds people with God and with one another, and Isaiah's plea for the quiet faith of the humble, who walk with God. It begins with justice. The 'doing of justice' was a central concern for the Old Testament Prophets.

In the New Testament, Jesus makes the practice of love and justice the very criterion for salvation: I was hungry and you gave me food … whatever you do to the least of my brothers and sisters that you do unto me (Mt 25:31-46). The beatitudes have justice and peace as the central theme. They point to the poor, the peacemakers and those who suffer in the cause of right: 'Blessed are the poor in spirit, the kingdom of heaven is theirs' (Mt 5:1-12). In our commitment to justice and peace, we know that God cares about the poor, that Christ is present in their midst and that we are called to do our best to help them.

The call of Christ covers the personal, the interpersonal and also the social, public side of our lives; the latter has to do with our place in society and community and how we structure these. It has become clear that a concern for justice and peace flows from love for others; love leads on to concern for others, respect for others, providing for their needs and making sure that each person's dignity and rights are safeguarded. This means that the call to work for justice, peace, and respect for creation belong at the heart of Christian commitment. As the African Synod document tells us: 'It is a Christian duty to bring to bear upon the social fabric an influence aimed at changing not only ways of thinking but also the very structures of society itself.'[16]

*Please read the following slowly and prayerfully and ask God to help you to experience the healing touch of his loving presence, so that you can act justly, love tenderly and walk humbly with your God. Remember that 'the fruit of silence is prayer. The fruit of prayer is faith. The fruit of faith is love. The fruit of love is service. The fruit of service is [justice and] peace (Mother Teresa).*

*Amos 5:21-25*
*(The prophets Micah and Amos had a great passion for social justice and abhorrence of religious ritual while justice was being ignored.)*
I hate, I despise your festivals, and I take no delight in your solemn assemblies. Even though you offer me your burnt offerings and grain offerings, I will not accept them; and the offerings of well-being of your fatted animals I will not look upon. Take away from me the noise of your songs; I will not listen to the melody of your harps. But let justice roll down like waters, and righteousness like an ever-flowing stream.

*James 3:13-18*
Who is wise and understanding among you? Show by your good life that your works are done with gentleness born of wisdom. But if you have bitter envy and selfish ambition in your hearts, do not be boastful and false to the truth. Such wisdom does not come down from above, but is earthly, un-spiritual, and devilish. For where there is envy and selfish ambition, there will also be disorder and wickedness of every kind. But the wis-

---

16. *The Church in Africa*, 54.

dom from above is first pure, then peaceable, gentle, willing to yield, full of mercy and good fruits, without a trace of partiality or hypocrisy. And a harvest of righteousness is sown in peace for those who make peace.

*Psalm 85:*
*(Righteousness (justice) and peace are the fruit of God's steadfast love)*

Restore us again, O God of our salvation,
and put away your indignation toward us.
Will you not revive us again,
so that your people may rejoice in you?

Show us your steadfast love, O Lord,
and grant us your salvation.
Let me hear what God the Lord will speak,
for he will speak peace to his people,
to his faithful, to those who turn to him in their hearts.

Steadfast love and faithfulness will meet;
righteousness and peace will kiss each other.
Faithfulness will spring up from the ground,
and righteousness will look down from the sky.

The Lord will give what is good,
and our land will yield its increase.
Righteousness will go before him,
and will make a path for his steps.

## 6.6. A grateful heart

The experience of Christ's love moves us to be grateful. A grateful heart manifests itself in a deep sensitivity to the needs of others, especially in their suffering. Gratitude is part of the unbreakable bond between love of God, love of self, love of others, and respect for God's creation. Gratitude is the heart of prayer. And gratitude is the memory of the heart. Gratitude is central to 'going the heart's way'. There is no more pleasing prayer on earth than a grateful heart. So we need to spend time in the area of gratitude, thankfulness and gratefulness. We can look back in anger and disappointment or we can look back in gratitude. We can be grateful for what we have or we can be resentful of others.

When I was in Kenya, there was something that always amazed me. The people are gifted at praying spontaneously and very often their prayer is a prayer of gratitude. They thank God for the gift of life, for good health, for the rains when they come, for the good harvest and so much more. They endure enormous suffering and do not have much of the material things in life, but thankfulness to God seems to come very naturally to them.

This is the way it was with Mary and Simeon and Zechariah. The first two chapters of St Luke's gospel contain some beautiful prayers. We get Mary's *Magnificat*; Zechariah's *Benedictus*; the message of the angels; and Simeon's *Nunc Dimittis*. These are wonderful prayers. They are full of gratitude and thankfulness for what God has done. They also express deep feelings of joy and gladness. These prayers can help us. We too are moved to be thankful and joyful for what the Lord has done and is doing for us in our daily lives, as we journey deeper into the mystery of his love for us. Ask God to help you to experience gratitude and joy in your heart. You can use the prayers from the first chapters of Luke to express your gratitude and joy.

*Please read the following prayers slowly and prayerfully and ask God to give you the gift of a grateful heart.*

*Two beautiful prayers of gratitude*
*1. Mary's Magnificat:*
My soul magnifies the Lord,
and my spirit rejoices in God my Saviour,
for he has looked with favour on the lowliness of his servant.
Surely, from now on all generations will call me blessed;
for the Mighty One has done great things for me,
and holy is his name.
His mercy is for those who fear him
from generation to generation.
He has shown strength with his arm;
he has scattered the proud in the thoughts of their hearts.
He has brought down the powerful from their thrones,
and lifted up the lowly;
he has filled the hungry with good things,
and sent the rich away empty.
He has helped his servant Israel,
in remembrance of his mercy,
according to the promise he made to our ancestors,
to Abraham and to his descendants forever' (Lk 1:46-55).

*2. Zechariah's Benedictus*
Blessed be the Lord God of Israel,
for he has looked favourably on his people and redeemed them.
He has raised up a mighty saviour for us
in the house of his servant David,
as he spoke through the mouth of his holy prophets from of old,
that we would be saved from our enemies
and from the hand of all who hate us.
Thus he has shown the mercy promised to our ancestors,
and has remembered his holy covenant,
the oath that he swore to our ancestor Abraham,
to grant us that we,
being rescued from the hands of our enemies,
might serve him without fear,
in holiness and righteousness before him all our days.
And you, child, will be called the prophet of the Most High;

for you will go before the Lord to prepare his ways,
to give knowledge of salvation to his people
by the forgiveness of their sins.
By the tender mercy of our God,
the dawn from on high will break upon us,
to give light to those who sit in darkness
and in the shadow of death,
to guide our feet into the way of peace' (Lk 1:68-79).

## 6.7. Hold on to hope

To live the unbreakable bond of love, we need hope that is anchored in God. It is easy to begin to lose hope, when we are confronted with the great sea of human suffering that surrounds us. When we are confronted with great suffering in our own lives or in the lives of family and friends, we can feel very helpless. From some of the surveys that have been carried out, it is clear that in these days a significant number of people experience this sense of helplessness and hopelessness. This can vary enormously. It covers a range of experience from the full force of despair, which sometimes ends in suicide, to the general feeling of discouragement that is less distressing but much more common. The latter can be part of the ordinary 'up and downs' of life. The reasons for the sense of hopelessness are complex. Professional help is often needed to unravel these. The support of family and friends is always crucial.

Many people draw strength from their hope in God's loving presence with them; this can be a source of great comfort. The scriptures and the scripture scholars can help us here. I find a book by Fr Wilfrid Harrington OP very helpful. The title of the book is: *Hold on the Hope – the Foolishness of God.*[17]

Hosea 11: 1-9 is one of the passages that Father Harrington reflects on in his book. He sees Hosea presenting God as a loving parent who never gives up on the children. No matter how the children behave God always remains loving and faithful, because God is God, not a human being. Fr Harrington traces this message through the Old Testament and into the New Testament. He shows there is a remarkably consistent pattern. On the one hand the prophets are condemning and criticising people's sinfulness and unfaithfulness; on the other hand, the central message in all the great prophets is always the same: God is loving, God is merciful, God is forgiving, God is faithful. This, of course, is the message of Christ himself. It is the basis of our hope.

---

17. Wilfrid Harrington OP, *Hold on the Hope – the Foolishness of God*, Dominican Publications, Dublin, 1998.

Fr Harrington assures us that God goes on doing this to the extent that we can talk about 'The foolishness of God' – this is the subtitle of his book. God goes on loving us even when we are unfaithful and ungrateful. We pray for a deep experience of this great mystery of God's infinite love and mercy. This will bring us hope, and enable us to go on loving when it is difficult and costly. It will enable us to keep 'going the heart's way' with great fortitude in times of trouble and distress.

*Please read this passage from Hosea and the hymn slowly and prayer-fully and ask God to fill you with faith in God's love and mercy and the hope that this brings.*

*Hosea 11:1-9*

When Israel was a child, I loved him, and out of Egypt I called my son. The more I called them, the more they went from me; they kept sacrificing to the Baals, and offering incense to idols. Yet it was I who taught Ephraim to walk, I took them up in my arms; but they did not know that I healed them. I led them with cords of human kindness, with bands of love. I was to them like those who lift infants to their cheeks. I bent down to them and fed them. They shall return to the land of Egypt, and Assyria shall be their king, because they have refused to return to me. The sword rages in their cities, it consumes their oracle-priests, and devours because of their schemes. My people are bent on turning away from me. To the Most High they call, but he does not raise them up at all. How can I give you up, Ephraim? How can I hand you over, O Israel? How can I make you like Admah? How can I treat you like Zeboiim? My heart recoils within me; my compassion grows warm and tender. I will not execute my fierce anger; I will not again destroy Ephraim; for I am God and no mortal, the Holy One in your midst, and I will not come in wrath.

*Psalm 65*
*(Our hope is based on God's bountiful love and goodness)*

> Praise is due to you, O God, in Zion;
> O you who answer prayer!
> To you all flesh shall come.
> When deeds of iniquity overwhelm us,
> you forgive our transgressions.
>
> Happy are those whom you choose
> and bring near to live in your courts.
> We shall be satisfied with the
> goodness of your house, your holy temple.
> By awesome deeds you answer us with deliverance.
>
> O God of our salvation,
> you are the hope of all the ends of the earth
> and of the farthest seas.
> You visit the earth and water it, you greatly enrich it;
> the river of God is full of water,
> you provide the people with grain,
> for so you have prepared it.
>
> You crown the year with your bounty;
> your wagon tracks overflow with richness.
> The pastures of the wilderness overflow,
> the hills gird themselves with joy,
> the meadows clothe themselves with flocks,
> the valleys deck themselves with grain,
> they shout and sing together for joy.

PART TWO

# *Living in these changing times*
### *'Going the heart's way' with prayer and discernment*

Our soul is waiting for the Lord,
The Lord is our help and our shield.
In him do our hearts find joy.
We trust in his holy name.
May your love be upon us, O Lord,
As we place all our trust in you.
*(Psalm 33)*

## I. Living in these changing times

There is a story about a white explorer in Africa, around the middle of the nineteenth century. He had collected a vast amount of goods, and he wanted to transport them back to Europe. But first he had to get them to the port, which was some distance away. He engaged a number of the local people to perform the task. One morning they set off, with each person carrying some of the goods. They travelled for a number of days, singing and dancing as they went. They were getting close to their destination and then one morning everything was silent – no singing, no dancing, no sound and there was no movement. The explorer tried everything to find out what was wrong, but all to no avail. Finally, he decided to sit among them. After some time he asked the man beside him what was wrong. He replied: 'We are waiting till our souls catch up.' They felt they had lost touch with their own world and their own souls. They had moved away from their familiar landscape, both physically and spiritually. They had gone too far, too fast. Sitting there, waiting in silence, was their way to 'go the soul's way' and to 'go the heart's way.'

This story can serve as a parable for life today, as people try to cope with the rapid changes that are taking place. For those of us who can look back forty years or more, we can hardly believe how much things have changed in that time. Our generation has seen more change than any number of previous generations put together. There is also a sense that the pace of change has accelerated in recent years. The last six months of 2008 have been particularly dramatic, with financial turmoil and so many people losing their jobs. People who had seen their fortunes improve rapidly have to cope with an even more rapid deterioration.

With so much happening so quickly, it is not surprising that we find ourselves trying to catch up. Our souls, our hearts, and even our bodies, have difficulty keeping up with the changes that are taking place. Like the people in the story, we may find ourselves going too far, too fast. We may need to follow their example, and stop occasionally, waiting in silence for our souls and our hearts to catch up.

The songwriter Brendan Graham, who wrote the song: *You Raise me up*, and a host of other hits in recent years, says: 'What worries me is that everything seems geared to the economy. We are not looking at what kind of society we want. I've often said, half jokingly, that there should be two new (government) ministries, a ministry of vision and a ministry for stillness and silence.' His world in Co Mayo seems to have plenty solitude: 'I feel most at home in the west. I love the isolation and serenity ... I am looking out at Lough Mask, the mountain is behind me and there is silence. I ponder the great questions like everyone else ... I go to a rock above Maamtrasna, just to sit, but sometimes things present themselves. Maybe it's the stillness, maybe it's not in the rocks but deep within.'[18] This is a man very much in touch with nature and with the landscape of the heart and soul, in the silence and stillness. His wonderful songs are imbued with deep spiritual insights that appeal to people all over the world. They have touched the hearts of many and helped them 'to go the heart's way.'

### The 'Desert' and the 'Oasis'

Pope Benedict talked about a 'desert' when he expressed his concern about the arid emptiness of Western culture, an emptiness that extends from the personal loneliness of individuals, all the way to destruction and desolation of the environment. 'The external deserts are growing,' he said, in his first papal pronouncement, 'because the internal deserts have become so vast.'

An image that is associated with the desert suggests itself here – the image of the 'Oasis.' The Oasis is a very powerful

---

18. In an interview in *The Irish Times*, 20 December 2007.

image for people who live in desert lands. For the traveller in the desert there are few comforts. Hour after hour of trudging through the lonely desert sands takes its toll; it leaves one longing for water, shade and rest; this is exactly what the oasis provides. The Oasis is the little fertile area in the desert, where life is preserved, nourished and sustained. With a visit to the Oasis the traveller is refreshed, renewed and strengthened for the rest of the journey.

We can use the image of the 'Oasis' to capture what will help us to keep in touch with the spiritual world. We are on the journey of faith, a journey into the mystery of God. We have to travel by way of the heart and soul and feel our way. Like the travellers in the desert, it will help us if we take time, at intervals, to be refreshed, restored and strengthened for the Journey. Perhaps we can visit a little 'Oasis' of quiet time in the way that the desert travellers visited the real one. This will mean that we come aside and rest awhile, so that we are refreshed and strengthened on our pilgrim way. If we can manage to do this, it will help us to stay in touch with what is deep within our hearts and souls; it will help us 'to go the heart's way'.

### Taking a 'Breather'

Spending quiet time in personal prayer in the course of the day can also be described as taking a 'breather.' In his wonderful book, *Travelling Light*, Daniel O'Leary presents thirty 'Breathers'. This word has been familiar to me from a young age. In my early teens, I spent much time working in the fields with my father and brothers. The work was hard and the hours were long. But at regular intervals, my father would say: 'We'll take a breather.' This meant taking time to rest and to relax. We could sit and enjoy the scenery and chat for ten or fifteen minutes. It was something we really appreciated. It restored us and enabled us to keep going. In a sense, it gave us time to breathe.[19]

We could say that the people in the African story were taking

---

19. My father had his own reason for these 'Breathers' – it may not have been good for his breathing; he loved his pipe and longed for a smoke!

a 'breather,' even if it was a rather long one! They were taking time to catch their breath, waiting for their souls and hearts to catch up. In our language, this is what personal prayer is about. It enables us to keep in touch with the spiritual world of our souls and our hearts, with spiritual values and a spiritual vision. We need this to keep in close contact with our spiritual home. If we move out and move too far away, we begin to feel out of touch with God, sensing his silence and feeling his absence.

# II. 'Going the heart's way'

### 'Going the heart's way' with respect for the mystery

As we 'go the heart's way,' people like St Augustine encourage us to have great respect for the mystery. Even though God is near us, with us and in us, God is ultimately beyond us, as the infinite and eternal mystery. There is a little story attributed to St Augustine that can help us here. It goes something like this. One day he was contemplating the mystery of God as he walked along a beach. At some stage he noticed a young boy digging a hole in the sand. He watched him for a while. When he had dug deeply, he grabbed his small bucket and ran to the water's edge. He quickly put some water in the bucket and rushed back to where the hole was. He poured the water into the hole and then took off again. He ran back and forth several times carrying small amounts of water in the bucket and pouring it into the hole. After some time Augustine asked him what he was doing. And as he took off once more for the water's edge, he replied that he was trying to empty the water of the ocean into the hole. Augustine was somewhat amused at the boy's innocence, but later found that the incident gave him an insight into what he himself was trying to do. The story became a kind of parable to describe what was happening when he tried to grasp the mystery of God with his human mind and express it in human words. He realised that he had as little chance of doing this, as the boy had of emptying the water of the vast ocean into the hole in the sand.

### 'Going the heart's way' in faith and silent love

In *The Spiritual Canticle* of St John of the Cross, we read: 'My beloved is the mountains and the lovely wooded valleys ... the whistling of love-stirring breezes, the tranquil night at the time of the rising dawn, silent music, sounding solitude, the supper that refreshes and deepens love.' And he encourages us to be 'silent before this great God, for the language he hears best is silent love'.

It is clear that St John was deeply in touch with the mystery of God in the world of nature, and that, for him, silence and love are the language of the heart – the spark that makes our ordinary humdrum lives light up with God. This is what happens for us when we journey in faith and love – 'going the heart's way'. We can feel God's presence and experience his light and love in the midst of life. There are traces of God everywhere. All around us we find the work of God's heart, as well as God's hands. If we take time to look and listen, we can feel the touch of mystery and glimpse the presence of the Divine.

Sometimes the sense of God's nearness can be strong and we can feel God's presence in a definite way, while at other times there is only a whisper or touch of God. This is the way it is. Much of the time, God's loving presence is being revealed in a quiet way in our hearts, in our souls, in our lives and in our world. St Paul assures us that the love of God has been poured into our hearts, through the Holy Spirit that has been given to us (Rom 5:5).

### 'Going the heart's way' with prayer

Prayer opens our hearts to the mystery of God in the ordinary events and experiences of life. It helps us to discern the touch of God's hand in the moments when we are peaceful and happy. It also helps us to realise that God is with us in times of darkness. This sometimes comes later. Prayer enables us to recognise God's presence in those who love us and in those who need us. Prayer is present when we pause and contemplate the mystery of God that surrounds us in creation. More often than not, we are filled with a deep sense of wonder and awe as we come face to face with the creator. We can feel God's closeness in the stillness.

St Teresa of Avila describes prayer as: 'Nothing else than a close sharing between friends; it means taking time frequently to be alone with him, who we know loves us.' A close sharing between friends is something that we experience in ordinary life. And the need to take time frequently to be alone with one who loves us is something that we are very much aware of. We also know from experience that the heart and feelings are central to friendship and sharing. So too in our friendship with God, we have to feel our way and 'go the heart's way'. This is why the heart is so central to prayer, and feeling our way is so important.

We do not need to say more prayers and longer prayers. We do not need to travel long distances on pilgrimage to find God. We simply need to take time frequently to be in the Lord's loving presence. This can be done wherever we are. The story of Martha and Mary encourages us to take time to be with Jesus. Mary sat at the feet of Jesus and she had chosen the better part. She had chosen to spend time with Jesus, face to face, as with a good friend. She was in a sacred space where she could enter into the heart of the mystery of Christ's loving presence. While Mary had chosen the better part, I am sure that Martha was also very close to Jesus, in the midst of her busy fretful life.

With the help of the Spirit, prayer is possible for everyone. It is not reserved for special people in special places. God can give the gift of prayer to anyone, at any time, in any place and at any age. The Spirit prays in us: 'The Spirit helps us in our weakness for, when we do not know how to pray as we ought, that very Spirit intercedes with sighs too deep for words. And God, who searches the heart, knows what is the mind of the Spirit …' (Rom 8:26-27).

With the help of the Spirit, we can pray, nourishing the spark of the divine in the heart and soul and spirit with a few lines of scripture or with whatever is required at a particular time. And, with the help of the Spirit, our prayer moves to loving in daily living. Genuine prayer and loving action belong together. In this way, faith and life merge. Mother Teresa summed it up: The fruit of silence is prayer. The fruit of prayer is faith. The fruit of faith is love. The fruit of love is service. The fruit of service is peace.

## 'Going the heart's way' with images and symbols

Thoughts and words are very limited when it comes to mystery and 'going the heart's way'. The affective, experiential area of life has much more to offer. This is where images and symbols, as well as parables and metaphors, come in. They help us to express and experience something of the mystery of God. They touch and reach into feelings and emotions in a way that human thinking can never do. They engage the heart, the soul, the spirit and the whole being. They help us to feel our way towards God.

Jesus himself used images and parables on many occasions. He spoke about the spring of living water, the light of the world and the salt of the earth. He drew many of his images from the world of nature: the birds of the air, the flowers of the field, the seed planted in the soil – to mention just a few.

The psalms are particularly rich in images and symbols. They are ideal for personal prayer and of course are at the centre of the church's liturgical prayer. The psalms give us a language to channel our feelings, as they help us to raise our hearts to God. They cover the whole range of human feelings, from praising God with our every breath, to expressing deep feelings of anguish, sadness, fear, and even despair.

While images and symbols are most helpful, they have their own complications if we take them too literally. We can see this when we reflect on some of the images and symbols for God that we find in scripture. God is like the rock and the spring of living water; God is pictured as a lion and an eagle; God is presented as a potter and a warrior; God is a merciful father and a caring mother. God is like a woman searching for a lost coin and like a shepherd searching for a lost sheep.

When we use these images we need to be aware of their limitations. God is a father in a certain sense – God is a good father, a merciful father, in the way that we know and experience human fatherhood. And even this is still limited. If we take it too literally we may end up disappointed. In one sense God is a father as we know fatherhood, but in another sense God is very different.

As well as using metaphors and images from scripture, we

can also come up with images from our own experience and
inner life. Poetry, literature, art and music are a great source of
images and symbols.

Despite the limitations, using images and symbols is one of
the best ways we have to express and experience something of
the infinite mystery of God. They are a great help to us as we try
to 'feel our way towards God' by 'going the heart's way'.

### 'Going the heart's way' through selfless giving

We have to guard against making absolute statements about the
way to God. Not only is God the infinite mystery, but the way to
God is also shrouded in mystery. In a sense, each person finds
his or her own way to God.

Having quiet time is important for 'going the heart's way'
but sometimes it may not be there in a person's life. Due to the
endless demands of family life and work commitments, silence
and solitude are often hard to find in daily living. Yet the journey to God continues for people who find themselves in this situation. The great writer Carlo Carretto noted that while he made
the journey to God in the silence of the desert, his mother made
the same journey in her busy life at home, rearing a large family.
The love of God flowed freely in her heart and life. She went the
'heart's way' through selfless giving. Her life and her prayer
flowed into each other, with little time for silence.

The 'quiet time' should not become another chore on top of
an already crowded schedule. On those days when life does not
allow you to stop, simply remember that God is present with
you in the midst of your daily life. Just try to welcome and ac-
knowledge God's presence in the opportunities for selfless giving. Then you are into prayer as you begin to recognise the
small, still voice of God in your busy world.

### 'Going the heart's way' in pain and suffering

Another situation can arise, when you have plenty of quiet time,
but you find it hard to pray. This can happen when you feel
weighed down with cares and worries, or you may be strug-

gling to cope with suffering. Pain and suffering can be so debilit-
ating and can leave us with little energy or enthusiasm for
prayer. When we find ourselves in this situation, we are advised
to remember that God is with us, in our darkest hours, when our
souls are weary and our hearts are troubled. God is with us in
the crosses and complexities of life, and is inviting us to be
aware of what is going on, and perhaps utter the simple prayer
of the blind man in the gospels: 'Lord, take pity on me' or 'Lord,
be merciful to me.' There are many simple invocations that were
favourite prayers of previous generations: 'Sacred Heart of
Jesus, I place my trust in you,' or 'Come to me and save me, Lord
God Almighty.' If we manage to say these simple prayers, and
keep repeating them, we are praying, and we may begin to
glimpse the Divine presence in the pain and anguish that are
part of everyone's life at some stage. When we are down beneath our burdens perhaps some comfort can be drawn from St
Augustine's picture of God hovering in love over the fragments
of our brokenness, and hovering in mercy over the dark and
storm-tossed waters of our tears and troubles.

## III. *Images for Personal Prayer*

### 1. The Seven Circles of Prayer

I find this image of seven circles very helpful. It is used in a thirty-minute video (and booklet) produced by the Housetop International Centre in London. John Wijngaards, the director of the Centre, came up with the image and developed it. It is based on the idea that, while each person travels his or her unique path to God, there are common elements that are found in everyone's prayer journey. The video presents these elements in terms of seven concentric circles through which everyone passes on the journey to God.

Prayer begins in *silence* (the first circle of prayer) and requires that we create *space* for it in our day. It opens our eyes and helps us to *see* things and people more deeply – with the eyes of faith, with the eyes of the heart. It opens us to so that we can hear the cry of *suffering* in others and ourselves. Prayer enables us to reach out and *touch* other people. It helps us to *listen* with the heart to God's Word in the Bible, and to God communicating with us in our ordinary lives. Everything in prayer leads up to and centres on a personal encounter of the heart with Christ, in whom we meet God *face to face*. This is the seventh circle of prayer. It is the circle at the very centre of prayer. You can see the Seven Circles in the diagram opposite.

The video stresses that prayer helps us to open our hearts to the mystery of God in the most ordinary things and in the ordinary events and experiences of life. It helps us to be aware of the mystery of God's loving presence, as it is being revealed to us in so many ways but especially as it comes to us through Christ our Saviour. Prayer opens our hearts to a personal encounter with Christ, our Saviour.

In the Seven Circles of Prayer we get good insights into what we mean by 'Going the heart's way'.

## The Seven Circles of Prayer[20]

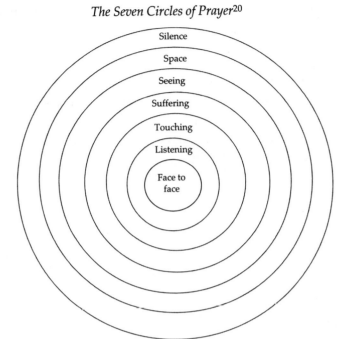

Silence

Space

Seeing

Suffering

Touching

Listening

Face to face

### 2. A close sharing between friends

'Contemplative prayer as nothing else than a close sharing between friends; it means taking time frequently to be alone with him, who we know loves us.'[21]

### 3. A Migrating Bird

The writer Evelyn Underhill used the image of a migrating bird to describe prayer. Even tiny birds can travel hazardous journeys of thousands of miles following their own inner radar. They are following an instinct placed in them by their creator. Like the migrating bird, we too have an inner instinct or restlessness. And this drives us on and draws us, like a magnet, deeper and further into the mystery of God. There is a spark of the divine and a deep desire for God in the human heart. St Augustine expressed it so beautifully when he prayed: 'You have made us

---

20. *The Seven Circles of Prayer* is available in DVD from: Housetop, 111A High Street, Rickmansworth, WD3 1AN, UK.
21. St Teresa of Avila, quoted in *CCC*, 2709.

for yourself, O Lord, and our hearts are restless until they rest in thee.'

### 4. A gaze of faith

'Contemplative Prayer is a gaze of faith fixed on Jesus. "I look at him and he looks at me" – this is what a certain peasant of Ars used to say to the holy Curé of Ars about his prayer before the tabernacle. This focus on Jesus is a renunciation of self. His gaze purifies our hearts; the light of his countenance illumines the eyes of our hearts and teaches us to see everything in the light of his truth and his compassion for all people' (CCC 2715).

### 5. The living water – Ways to water a garden.[22]

According to St Teresa of Avila, anyone who wants to learn how to pray should imagine that he or she is going to make a garden for the Lord, and this in a place where the soil is barren and weeds grow in plenty. It is the Lord himself who plucks up the weeds and puts in good plants. It is then for us, by God's grace, like good gardeners, to make these plants grow. We must water them carefully so that they may not wither but will bear blossoms that will give forth a fragrance pleasing to God. She says that the garden can be watered in four different ways.

Firstly, by drawing water from the well, at the cost of heavy labour. Secondly, by using a water wheel (pump) and buckets. (She said she had done this herself sometimes, and it brings more water with less fatigue.) Thirdly, by a stream or brook, which is better still, for the soil is thoroughly saturated, the gardener's labour is less, and water is not needed so often; Fourthly, by a downpour of rain, and this last is by far the best; for the Lord himself waters the garden without any aid from us.

She then uses these four ways of watering a garden to explain the four degrees of prayer in which the Lord in his goodness had sometimes placed her soul.

---

22. St Teresa of Avila, *The Book of her Life*, chapter 11 and following, *The Collected Works of St Teresa of Avila*, trs Kieran Kavanaugh OCD and Otilio Rodriguez OCD. ICS Publications, Washington DC, 1976.

## 6. The Three Circles – Prayer, Love and Justice[23]

We can use this image to indicate the connection between prayer, love and Justice. Donal Dorr uses the image to illustrate the three dimensions of an integral or balanced spirituality. Prayer is an essential part of such spirituality. But it is always seen in connection with the other dimensions. The scripture text used for the circles is Micah 6:8: This is what the Lord your God asks of you: to act justly, to love tenderly, and to walk humbly with your God. The three circles are interlocking as follows:

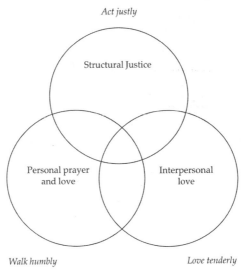

*Act justly*

Structural Justice

Personal prayer
and love

Interpersonal
love

*Walk humbly*                                          *Love tenderly*

Each circle represents a dimension of spirituality. The first circle (with 'Walk Humbly' beside it) represents the personal area of humble faith in God. Prayer, in which we walk humbly with God, fosters this but it also fosters love and justice in the areas represented by the other two circles.

The second circle (with 'Love Tenderly' beside it) represents the interpersonal area, which is lived out in the tender love of others. The third circle (with 'Act Justly' beside it) represents the public area, which expresses itself in concern for justice and human rights. It also covers respect for creation and the environment. All three dimensions belong together in spirituality. Thus

23. Donal Dorr, *Integral Spirituality*, Gill and MacMillan, Dublin, 1990, p 2.

prayer is never just a private, personal, isolated activity. It is always related to love in the interpersonal area, and to justice in the public area. There is an unbreakable bond between all these areas.

## 7. A Child of God

'Contemplative prayer is the prayer of the child of God, of the forgiven sinner who agrees to welcome the love by which he is loved and who wants to respond to it by loving even more. But he knows that the love he is returning is poured out by the Spirit in his heart, for everything is grace from God. Contemplative prayer is the poor and humble surrender to the loving will of the Father in ever deeper union with his beloved Son' (*CCC* 2712).

## 8. Beside the Well

'The wonder of prayer is revealed beside the well where we come seeking water: there, Christ comes to meet every human being. It is he who first seeks us and asks us for a drink. Jesus thirsts; his asking arises from the depths of God's desire for us. Whether we realise it or not, prayer is the encounter of God's thirst with ours. God thirsts that we may thirst for him.' (*CCC* 2560).

## 9. The solitude of the mountains[24]

'In so far as contemplative prayer is a temporary ceasing from our external activity, work and various ministries, this ceasing is only to equip us all the better to return to them with mind, heart and body renewed. We ponder in silence, in the sands of the spirit, only so as to be surer of the way we walk on the streets of life when we return. We enter into the solitude of the mountains from our travels in the busy valley, so as to see more clearly and with perspective, the hidden hazards and the potential wrong turnings of those travels. Jesus took his disciples aside to a quiet place, on occasion, so as to purify and intensify the spirit that animated their intense apostolate ...

---

24. Daniel J. O' Leary, *Travelling Light*, The Columba Press, Dublin, 2001, p 200.

If, then, we make this contemplative habit of mind and heart like second nature to us, the time we spend alone with God in personal prayer will be rich and transforming.'

## 10. The 'Oasis'

As we noted earlier, the oasis is a very powerful image for people who live in desert lands. For the traveller in the desert, there are very few comforts. Hour after hour of trudging through the lonely desert sands takes its toll; it leaves one longing for water, shade and rest and this is exactly what the oasis provides. The oasis is that little fertile area in the desert, where life is preserved, nourished and sustained. The visitor to the oasis is refreshed, renewed and strengthened for the rest of the journey.

We can use the image of the oasis to capture much of what is involved in our periods of personal prayer. As travellers on the journey into the mystery of God, we take time, at intervals, to be refreshed, restored, and strengthened for the journey. We need the oasis of personal prayer in the way that the desert travellers need the real one. We need to come aside and rest awhile, so that we are refreshed and strengthened on our pilgrim way to God.

## IV. Discerning the Divine Presence [25]

In his book, *Beyond Personality*, C. S. Lewis describes how an old army officer challenged him during a lecture on the Trinity. He stood up in the middle of the crowded hall and said: 'I've no use for all that stuff. But, mind you, I'm a religious man too. I know there is a God. I've felt him when I was out alone in the desert at night: I was aware of the tremendous mystery. And that's just why I don't believe all your neat little dogmas and formulas about God. To anyone who has met the real thing, they all seem so petty and pedantic and unreal.'

Lewis goes on to say that in a sense he agreed with the man. He felt that the man had a real experience of God in the desert. When he turned from that experience to theology, he was turning from something very real to something less real and less interesting. And then Lewis goes on to explain why discernment and the guidance coming from theology are important and relevant when we embark on the spiritual journey.

He uses the following image: Imagine a person on the beach on a beautiful summer day, looking out at the ocean, enjoying the sun, the sand and the sea. Later that same person looks at a map of the ocean. The experience of looking at the ocean from the beach and the experience of looking at it on the map are very different. The map is only coloured paper but there are two things that make the map relevant and important: 'In the first place, the map is based on what hundreds and thousands of people have found sailing the ocean; the map fits all the different experiences together. In the second place, if you want to go anywhere, the map is absolutely necessary.'

---

25. Discernment is a very important but also a very complex topic. It is not possible to give a detailed account of it in this short article. I can only make some general observations.

As long as we remain on the beach we can enjoy and experience the ocean. But if we decide to venture out on to the vast ocean, we will need a compass and a map. So too if we want to journey into the mystery of God, we need the insights of people who have travelled the journey ahead of us. We need to be able to find our bearings, especially when we encounter darkness and doubts along the way. These are part of the journey, as we sometimes find we are groping to find our way, like a driver in the fog. At such times we need to be able to discern the divine presence.

### Discerning the Divine Presence – The Heart of Prayer

As Christians, we believe that we are being 'led by the Spirit' and live a 'life in the Spirit' that is at home in our heart (Rom 8:9). We know that 'those who live according to the Spirit set their minds on things of the Spirit' (Rom 8:5). We live with the promise: 'You will receive power when the Holy Spirit has come upon you, and you will be my witnesses' (Acts 1:8). And as he breathed on the disciples, he said: 'Receive the Holy Spirit, as the Father sent me, so I send you' (Jn 20:20-21). The Holy Spirit is working deep within us and within our lives, and within the whole of creation.

Discernment helps us to notice the various ways in which the Holy Spirit (that Christ promised) is present and active in our lives. A discerning heart is the key here. We have 'to go the heart's way'. Discernment is focused on human experience and on the human heart. The main words in discernment are: noticing, perceiving, feeling, inner movement and the inner life. We need to add that all sorts of external matters in life and relationships are also relevant, as well as theology, scripture and the tradition of the church.

St Ignatius used the Spanish word *sentir* when he described discernment. John Futrell writes: 'In the process of discernment, *sentir* comes to mean above all a kind of felt-knowledge, an affective, intuitive knowledge possessed through the reaction of human feelings to exterior and interior experience.'[26]

---

26. Quoted in Jules J Toner, *Discernment of Spirits,* Institute of Jesuit Resources, 1982, p 22.

This is a good description of what we mean by 'going the heart's way' and by 'feeling our way to God'. It involves felt knowledge that is affective and intuitive. This indicates that the heart is central in discernment, but the word 'intuitive' (the need to perceive with insight) indicates that the head too has its place. A little phrase sums it up: 'Trust your heart but also use your head as you feel your way.'

## Discernment: Love of Christ and love of others

Growth in love is the clearest indication that we are being 'led by the Spirit'. A discerning heart is very much a loving heart. For St Paul and St John, everything is subjected to love. In chapter thirteen of his first letter to the Corinthians, St Paul brings this out very clearly. He says that if he has all the gifts of men and of angels and he has faith to move mountains, even if he would give his body to be burnt, but has no love, then he is just a gong booming and a symbol clashing. And this is the love that comes from Christ. It is the love of Christ and love for Christ. It is the love of God (Christ) that has been poured into our hearts, by the Holy Spirit that has been given to us (Rom 5:5). So growth in the love of Christ is the key to discernment.

Furthermore, love of others is the true manifestation of our love of Christ; it may even be seen as the real test of such love: 'The truth of our union with Jesus Christ in the Eucharist is tested by whether or not we love our fellow men and women; it is tested by how we treat others' (*Pope John Paul II*).

It follows that a deepening of Christian faith and love is the best foundation for discernment, which is not just something that we switch on and off, when there is a choice or decision to be made, but something that helps us to feel our way all the time on our journey into the mystery of God. Thus the habit of discernment is anchored in our Christian commitment, deep within the mind and heart and soul of each person.

## The Fruits of the Spirit

The following advice that Jesus gives can help us with discernment: 'You will know them by their fruits. Are grapes gathered from thorns or figs from thistles? In the same way, every good tree produces good fruit and a rotten tree bad fruit. A good tree cannot bear bad fruit, nor can a bad tree bear good fruit ... you will know them by their fruits' (Mt 7:16-20).

We can express it this way: Anything that leads to hatred, bitterness, hostility and confusion cannot come from God, and anything that produces the fruits of the Spirit in the person's life is surely coming from God – and the fruits of the Spirit are these: 'Love, joy, peace, patience, kindness, generosity, faithfulness, gentleness and self-control' (Gal 5:22). There is good guidance here.

We also need to note the warning that Jesus gave about expecting extraordinary signs and wonders to authenticate his presence. When the Pharisees demanded that Jesus produce a miracle to prove that God was with him, Jesus refused: 'I tell you solemnly, no sign will be given to this generation' (Mk 8:12).

Jesus was impatient with the Pharisees who, as spiritual men, should have been able to discern spiritual signs. He expected them to perceive God's power and presence in him without attaching too much importance to external signs and wonders. He teaches us to be cautious about placing too much emphasis on these things, but to be sensitive to the presence of his Spirit working in our hearts and touching our lives and relationships: 'for the Spirit searches the depths of everything, even the depths of God.' (1 Cor 2:10).

With this kind of sensitivity to the Spirit, we will 'go the heart's way.'